Woman's Day
COOL CRAFTS

Over 200 Easy-to-Create Projects for the Whole Family

filipacchi
publishing

DIFFICULTY LEVELS

E EASY

I INTERMEDIATE

D DIFFICULT

Copyright © 2007 Filipacchi Publishing USA, Inc.

First published in the United States of America by
Filipacchi Publishing
1633 Broadway
New York, NY 10019

Crafts consultant: Michele Filon

Proofreading: Jennifer Ladonne

Design: Patricia Fabricant

ISBN: 1-933231-26-2

Printed in China.

CONTENTS

HALLOWEEN

BAT BAGS **E**

Spook your halls with these crafty creatures.

FOR EACH ONE

Lunch-size paper bag
Tacky glue (we used Aleene's Original)
Construction paper remnants
Two 10 mm movable eyes
12" of ¼" ribbon
Hole punch
Elastic cord

CUT slits two-thirds of the way down all four corners of a paper bag.

GLUE narrow side flaps together at the top. Cut ear shapes along upper edge.

CUT scalloped edges along wide flaps to create wings.

FOLD wings accordion-style.

CUT mouth and ears from construction paper.

GLUE on paper mouth and ears, movable eyes and a ribbon bow.

PUNCH hole between ears and thread through an elastic cord to make your bat fly.

BAT NECKLACE **E**

Scrap black Fun Foam
Scissors or craft knife
Assorted rhinestones
Fabric or jewel glue
Purple satin cord in desired length

CUT out bat shape, below, from foam.

GLUE on rhinestones.

MAKE holes in foam; thread on cord; knot cord ends together.

BAT-AND-MOON MOBILE

Heavy brown paper or grocery bag
Tacky glue (we used Aleene's Original)
Fiberfill stuffing or shredded paper
Acrylic paints: white, yellow and black
Paintbrushes
Brown liquid wax shoe polish
36" heavy black wire

ENLARGE patterns, right (see *How to Enlarge Patterns*, page 144).

CUT from brown paper, glue with tacky glue in pairs with scant ¼"-wide line of glue at edge, leaving opening for stuffing and opening at each dot for wire. Let dry. (Note: Can be speed-dried on low setting at short intervals in microwave; watch to prevent scorching.)

STUFF lightly with fiberfill or shredded paper. Glue opening closed.

PAINT bat black and moon yellow with acrylic paints. Let dry. Mix white and black paints to make gray. Paint gray bat face.

STREAK pieces with shoe polish and wipe off with a clean cloth for antiqued look.

GLUE wire into hole for hanging.

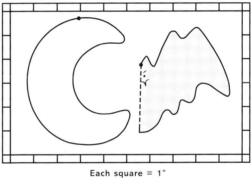

Each square = 1"

BROOMSTICK CREATURE

FOR EACH ONE

Broom
1 yd batting
1 yd fabric
Colored raffia
Cotton string
Trims, scraps of felt and buttons
Low-temp glue gun

WRAP batting around broom. Tie into place loosely with string.

CUT 1-yd square of fabric. Place center of fabric over broom and fold around, stretching tightly over batting. Wrap raffia around neck of broom; tie with string to hold. Trim off excess with scissors.

GLUE on buttons, scraps and trims for eyes and mouth.

CANDY CORN GANG Ⓓ

FOR EACH ONE

7" x 12" piece each orange and yellow fabric
Two each fabrics (or bias tape) 1" x 5" for arms,
  1" x 4" for legs
Two 12" or one 18" chenille stems
Fiberfill, beans or pellets for stuffing
Scraps of felt for boots
Optional for costumes: two 6" x 4" pieces fabric
  for cape
Scraps of fur or bandanna for hat
Black felt hat
Tiny paper treat bag
Brown paper and twine or wired paper for bag

TRACE patterns, right, for body top, bottom and boot.

CUT 2 tops from yellow or orange fabric and 2 bottoms from opposite color. Stitch each top to a bottom, with right sides together, ¼" seam allowance. Press open.

ARMS: Fold in ¼" on long edges and one end of fabric (tape is already folded). Fold in half lengthwise, right side out; topstitch ¹⁄₁₆" from long edges. Insert

4" chenille stem, leaving ¾" fabric free at top of arm. Baste arms to body front between lines at sides.

LEGS: Make as for arms, 4" long.

STITCH front to back along smooth curve of sides and top. At lower corners, stitch darts with dots each side together, to create boxed corners. Then stitch across lower edge, leaving 1½" open at center. Turn right side out.

INSERT and baste a leg into each end of opening. Stuff body firmly. Sew opening closed.

CUT felt boots; glue to legs.

PAINT face.

DRESS as you like.

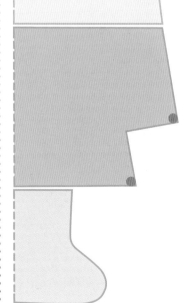

CAPE: Stitch two 6" x 4" pieces of fabric together, wrong side out, leaving an opening. Turn. Fold down ½" at top for casing; stitch ⅜" from fold. Insert ribbon; tie around neck.

PIRATE'S BANDANNA: Cut 10"-wide triangle off corner of a bandanna. Turn raw edge under. Tie around head, tucking in free corner; sew or glue in place.

CAT: Cut 2 fur pieces to fit across top of head; sew together leaving bottom open. Cut 2 small ears; tack to top. Tack hat to head. Cut 1½" x 7" strip for tail. Roll lengthwise and glue; glue to back. Add black-thread whiskers to face.

KITTY KAT KORNERED ❶

*Small (about 45 oz) bleach bottle for body and
    detergent bottle for head and ears; neck should
    fit closely in neck of bleach bottle (we used
    9" Dawn or Joy Non-Ultra)*
China marker or permanent felt tip
Black paint for plastic
Flat paintbrush
Tracing paper
Pinking shears
Fun Foam scraps: yellow and green
36" of white florist's wire; wire cutters
Low-temp glue gun
Two 10 mm movable eyes
2" x 10½" fabric for tie
Black chenille stem (optional)

WASH and dry bottles, removing labels. Remove caps.
Turn detergent bottle upside down; lower wedge section
with opening will become the cat's head. Draw ears on
front up from top of head using marker. Cut off bottle
around ears with scissors.

PAINT head and bleach bottle solid black as directed.
Let dry.

TRACE green nose and yellow mouth patterns printed
over text. Using pinking shears, cut mouth from foam.
Cut four 8" whiskers from wire.

GLUE eyes to head. Glue center of whiskers together
behind nose. Glue on mouth. Glue neck of head into
neck of body so that handle is at side as a tail.

CUT 1" off end of fabric strip. Fold ends of long strip to
meet at center back; wrap short strip around center to
form bow tie; glue closed. Glue tie to front of neck, or
insert chenille through back of center loop and fasten
around neck.

FAT CATS ❶

FOR EACH ONE

*Dry rice or beans for weight, plastic fold-top
    sandwich bag*
Fiberfill stuffing, scrap batting (optional)
Sock, any size
Thin string or strong thread
*Fun Foam scraps: ⅛"-thick in sock color for ears,
    yellow for nose, magenta or other color for eyes;
    ¼"-thick black or orange for hat*
Pinking shears
Craft knife, ruler, pencil
Low-temp glue gun
Fabric glitter spray (we used Tulip)
*Acrylic paints: black and color to match eyes
    (optional)*
Pointed paintbrush
2 chenille stems matching sock (for tail)
Yellow dimensional paint (we used Tulip Slick)
*12" of green
    florist's wire*
Wire cutters

FILL plastic bag with
1 or 2 handfuls rice.
Tie or tape closed.
Wrap with a thin layer
of stuffing or batting
and insert in toe of
sock. Stuff firmly to
desired size of cat;
tie with string; trim
excess flat.

TRACE rim of a cup
or glass for hat brim
on ⅛" foam with
pencil. Cut out with
pinking shears. Cut triangle for peak 3"–4" tall and 1"–
2" wide from ¼" foam using craft knife along ruler. Glue
peak upright to brim. Spray hat with glitter as directed.
Let dry. Glue to top of cat.

CUT 1" foam triangles for ears. Cut smaller yellow
triangle for nose and magenta ovals for eyes.

PAINT black pupils on eyes. Paint triangles or glue on
foam for inner ears matching eye color. Let dry. Glue
eyes, nose and ears to cat.

TWIST 2 chenille stems together for tail. Glue 1" at one
end to lower back. Bend and coil tail to show at side.

PAINT mouth with dimensional paint (practice first on
scrap paper). Let dry. Cut three 4" wires. Insert through
sock behind nose and muzzle for whiskers.

CAT ON THE HAT ①

Straw hat with rounded crown
Gesso (we used Krylon spray)
Acrylic paints (we used FolkArt Pure Black, Lemon
    Custard, Pure Orange, Metallic Amethyst)
Flat paintbrushes
Tracing paper
Tacky glue (we used Aleene's Quick Dry)
Lime and purple craft powder or glitter
Black, lime, orange and purple scraps of
    Fun Foam
Black fine-point permanent marker
Sparkle Spray (we used Tulip)
1 yd of white paper-wrapped wire for whiskers;
    large needle for wire; wire cutter
½ yd of giant black chenille for tail
3" of ¼"-wide ribbon
Ribbon for hanger (1 yd each ⅝"-wide purple
    and ⅞"-wide green grosgrain)
Stapler

SPRAY gesso on outside of hat. Let dry.

PAINT cat's head on crown and chest on brim black. Let dry. Paint one side of background yellow, the other orange, blending colors around the top.

TRACE ear, eye and nose patterns, below. Cut from foam. Working on a newspaper-protected surface, place small pieces on paper towels to catch powders or glitters. Apply glue then lime powder or glitter to eyes and purple to front of inner ears, reversing one each. Let dry.

GLUE pupils to eyes and inner ears to ears, reversing one ear. Score ears from front on dotted line to fold upright. Glue eyes, nose and ears to face.

PAINT yellow grinning mouth and metallic amethyst collar, following photo, left. Let dry. Cut ½" x 6½" purple foam strip for bow tie; lap and glue ends; flatten and glue center. Glue foam circle (trace a penny) to center front. Paint amethyst.

PRINT "Beware!" on background with marker; paint lettering black. Let dry.

SPRAY sparkles lightly over entire hat, following directions on can.

INSERT three 11" wires at one side of nose and out the other leaving ends each side as whiskers. Glue or staple chenille tail to front as shown, tucking lower end under hat brim.

HANGER: Hold 27" lengths of grosgrain ribbons together and tie in bow. Lap purple over remaining green ribbon and glue together; glue bow to one end. About 7" below bow attach ribbon to top back of hat with 2 staples. Trim excess. Fold 3" of the ¼"-wide ribbon in half with ends crossed; glue behind bow as hanging loop.

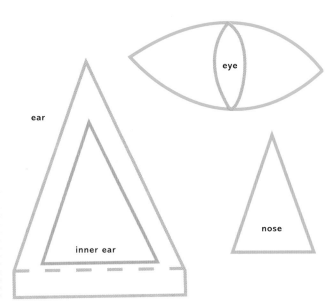

KITTY BANNER ❶

SIZE: *22" x 37"*

1 yd paper-backed fusible web
Cotton or cotton-blend fabrics:
 23" x 38" medium-weight black for background;
 three 17" x 15" Halloween prints for cats;
 6" x 23" strip white: scraps of yellow and white
1½ yds 1½"-wide black grosgrain ribbon
Black thread and straight pins
Three ¾" black pompoms
Six ⅜" colored buttons
Fabric glue (we used Fabri-Tac)
Dimensional fabric paints (we used white, black,
 orange and green Plaid Fashion Paint)
Dowel or curtain rod

ENLARGE patterns, below, for cat, picket points, stars and moon (see *How to Enlarge Patterns,* page 144).

IRON fusible web to back of appliqué fabrics, following manufacturer's directions. Trace 3 cats, reversing one. Working out from center, trace picket points along top edge of white fabric strip, moon and stars on yellow or white. Cut from fabrics. Peel off backing.

POSITION pieces on black fabric, with fence flush at bottom and cats stacked as shown.

PRESS under ½" on banner edges, folding corners neatly. Cut seven 7" ribbons for hanging loops; fold in half. Pin ½" ends to top back evenly spaced; topstitch around banner about ⅛" from edges with matching thread.

GLUE on pompom noses and button eyes.

PAINT over raw edges of cats in orange or green, stars and fence in black. (Practice using paint first and work from top down to avoid smearing.) Define pickets. Paint white whiskers, black lip line. Let dry. Hang banner from dowel or curtain rod.

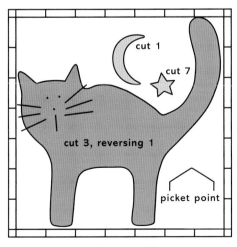

cut 1

cut 7

cut 3, reversing 1

picket point

Each square = 2"

PUMPKIN TOTEM ⓔ

10" x 13" piece of ¼" plywood for totem
Saber saw
Acrylic paints (we used Kelly Green, Pure Orange,
  Licorice, Christmas Red and Periwinkle FolkArt)
Round and flat brushes
5½" pine 1 x 4 for base
Sponge
Glue gun with wood-glue sticks
2" pine 1 x 2 for block
Scrap of raffia

CUT plywood totem from pattern, below, with saw (see *How to Enlarge Patterns,* page 144) or create your own design.

PAINT main colors. When dry, paint details.

PAINT base green, with orange striped sides. When dry, sponge top with black well blotted on a slightly damp sponge.

GLUE block to back, flush at bottom, as a support. Glue totem to center of base. Glue raffia bow below bat.

BEANBAG PUMPKINS ⓘ

Circles of orange fabric 10" to 18" in diameter
Quilting or other strong thread for gathering
Polyfill pellets or beans for filling
Small amount of fiberfill stuffing
Scraps of green fabric and ribbon for stem and
  leaves
Fabric glue
Green floral wire
ThermO Web PeelnStick double-side adhesive paper
Black fabric for features

PENCIL a circle about 2" in from edge on wrong side of fabric circle. Starting and ending on the right side, with doubled quilting thread, sew small running stitches on the line for gathering; turn right side out. Secure one end of thread.

PULL thread to gather, leaving a 4" opening. Fill halfway with beans or pellets; finish with fiberfill. Tighten gathers to close top; wind thread around excess to form stem.

CUT leaf shapes from ribbon or fabric. Glue at base of stem. Glue green fabric over stem, folding in edges. Curl green wire around a pencil and twist around base of stem to form tendrils.

DRAW pumpkin eyes, nose and mouth on back of the double-adhesive paper. Adhere black fabric. Cut out; peel off backing; place on pumpkin.

PUMPKIN TOTEM   Each square = 1"

CHENILLE PUMPKINS 🅘

FOR EACH ONE

3 orange 12" bump chenille stems
Low-temp glue gun
1 each yellow and green plain chenille stems
Two 10 mm movable eyes
¾" tip of wooden toothpick or skewer painted orange
1¼" circle of Fun Foam or cardboard

TWIST the 3 orange stems together firmly at centers (about 3 twists). Spread ends apart, then bend them in toward center, crossed at top. Glue tips to center to form a hollow ball. Shape so sides are evenly covered, and glue strands together at top where they cross.

BEND 1¼" pieces of yellow chenille into circles to hold eyes and border nose. Bend zigzag mouth. Glue in place. Glue on movable eyes and toothpick nose.

CUT 6" green chenille. Twist up ½" for stem and coil remainder; glue to pumpkin top. Glue foam circle to bottom for stand.

PUMPKIN FACES 🅔

White paper plates
Orange acrylic paint
Paintbrush
Craft glue
Black paper
Green paper leaves
Green chenille stems

PAINT the whole plate orange.

CUT features from black paper. Glue them on the plates (don't forget to dot the eyes), and top with two colored paper leaves and a squiggly green-chenille stem.

JACK-O'-LANTERNS ❶

Pumpkin-carving kit (contains saw-knife and scoop)
Black fine-point permanent marker or pen
Clay loop carving tool (available at most art supply stores)
Glitter paint
White scrap fabric
Chenille stems
Nails
Small votive candle or light stick

COVER work surface with newspaper.

DRAW a circle around pumpkin stem large enough for hand to fit through. With saw-knife, slant cuts inward toward the stem.

REMOVE insides with scoop.

DRAW on design for face with markers. If necessary use plastic lids or bowls as templates for circles (eyes, mouth).

CARVE out design using saw-knife in slow back-and-forth motion.

CREATE effects like eyebrows or "Boo" letters with clay loop tool by carving away surface of pumpkin.

PAINT stem with glitter paint. Let dry.

WRAP mummy pumpkin with strips of white fabric.

USE nail to make holes for adding chenille stem details.

SELECT a safe place to display pumpkin away from any object that may catch fire. Put small votive candle or light stick inside.

NEVER leave lit candles unattended.

ROLY-POLY PUMPKIN Ⓓ

SIZE: *About 20" diam*

> 9" x 18" paper
> 2 yds of 45"-wide muslin for lining
> White and orange sewing thread
> White buttonhole thread
> Fabric glue
> Thick fleece fabric (we used Polarfleece by Malden Mills): 1 yd of 54"-wide orange, 8½" x 12" piece green
> 2 large bags of plastic-foam pellets (from mailing-supply store) as filling
> 1 yd of ⅝" Velcro Soft & Flexible Sew-on Fastener Tape
> 2 white ⅜" Velcro sew-on coins
> Scraps of black felt
> Small amount of fiberfill stuffing

CUTTING: Enlarge pumpkin pattern, left (See *How to Enlarge Patterns,* page 144). Fold 9" x 18" paper in half lengthwise. Place section pattern on top, aligned at bottom and with vertical center line on fold. Cut along outer edge through both layers. Open flat for half section. Fold fabric in half crosswise and place bottom of half-pattern on fold. Cut 6 muslin sections. Cut 6 fleece sections, making edge of one section ¾" wider for flap (mark flap with safety pin).

LINING: Stitch muslin sections together, wrong side out, with ⅜" seam allowance, leaving a 10" opening. Clip curves. Turn right side out. Stuff with pellets. Sew firmly closed with buttonhole thread.

COVER: Turn under ⅜" on marked edge and edge of a section to adjoin it; stitch. Separate Velcro tape. Stitch one strip to wrong side of ¾" marked flap; stitch mate over edge of adjoining section. Close Velcro. Add remaining sections with ¼" seam allowance. Open Velcro. Turn. Insert stuffed lining.

FACE: Cut features from black felt. Glue or sew in place. Separate white coins. Cut small wedge in soft halves. Glue remainders to eyes.

STEM: Fold green fleece in half lengthwise, wrong side out; stitch end and side closed. Turn. Stuff with fiberfill. Turn under lower edge; sew firmly to top of pumpkin.

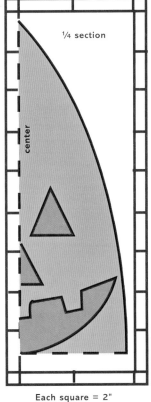

¼ section

center

Each square = 2"

PUMPKIN-FACE GARLAND

Six 7"-diam orange plastic or paper plates
  for each 42" length of garland
Black marker; small paintbrush
Black and white paint for plastic (for plastic plates)
  or acrylic paint (for paper plates)
Green Fun Foam
Tacky glue (we used Aleene's Quick Dry)
Hole punch
Scraps or ⅛ yd each orange, green, lavender and
  black fabrics; a few strands orange and black
  raffia
4 yds of black yarn for every 6 plates

OUTLINE jack-o'-lantern faces on back of plates with marker. Fill in with paint. Let dry. Add white highlights to eyes.

CUT pumpkin stems, about ¾" x 1½", from green foam. Punch hole centered at one end; glue other end to back of plate. Tie a 10" strand of yarn to the hole.

CUT 2" x 10" strips of fabric; trim ends diagonally.

LAY out about 78" yarn or desired length for garland, leaving 18" ends for tying. Working out from center, line up pumpkin plates below, touching side by side. Tie each plate to the strand to hang about 2" below yarn. Tie 3 ribbons or bunches of raffia between pumpkins and along ends of garland.

TENNIS BALL GANG

Old tennis balls
Acrylic paints (we used FolkArt White, Black,
  Glazed Carrots)
¾" stiff paintbrush for ball, fine brush for details
Assorted small hats
Tacky glue (we used Aleene's Quick Dry) or glue gun
Two 1" pompoms and scrap of felt for earmuffs

PAINT ball white. When dry, paint orange. Let dry.

PAINT simple, funny jack-o'-lantern faces with black and white paint. Let dry.

GLUE on hat. For earmuffs, glue felt strip across top and a pompom on each side.

PUMPKIN STACK

Seven ¼"-diam dowels: one 15½", six 4"
Craft knife, scissors, pencil or ¼"-diam scrap dowel
4 white plastic-foam balls, 1 each approx. 2", 4", 5"
*   and 6" diam*
Acrylic paints (we used FolkArt Pure Black, Pumpkin,
*   Terra Cotta, Hydrangea, Leaf Green, Sunny*
*   Yellow)*
1" flat paintbrush
Tracing paper
Glue for plastic foam (we used Aleene's Foamtastic)
Fun Foam scraps: ⅛"-thick black and white;
*   ¼"-thick orange and white (for ghosts)*
10 mm movable eyes
Dimensional paints (we used Plaid Dimensional
*   Fashion Fabric Shiny Purple, Shiny Orange,*
*   Neon Glo-in-the-Dark)*
Low-temp glue gun
1½ yds of green florist's wire; wire cutter
Foil or foam chunk as prop for drying

SHARPEN one end of 15½" dowel with craft knife. Carefully push dowel up through center of 6", 5" and 4" balls; remove dowel. With tip of paintbrush handle, score 9 or 10 evenly spaced shallow grooves running from top to bottom of each ball to define pumpkin segments. Smooth with side of handle.

PAINT 2" ball black for bat, paint larger balls pumpkin, inserting a dowel or pencil to hold ball while you paint. Prop in foam on pencils or in crumpled foil to dry. Shade grooves with terra-cotta. Let dry. Paint hydrangea, leaf green and sunny yellow stripes on 4" dowels for arms.

PUSH 6" ball down on a hard surface to flatten center bottom or cut off a small slice with a serrated knife. Glue pumpkins together on long dowel, leaving bottom flat and ½" pointed end at top to hold bat. Let dry. Mark sides slightly above pumpkin centers for arms. Glue arms in ½" deep, angling lower 4 arms upward.

TRACE patterns for pumpkin face, ghost, hand, bat wing, ear and tooth, below. Using scissors or craft knife, cut 3 different jack-o'-lantern faces from black foam; glue to front of pumpkins. Cut varied orange foam hands; glue to front of arms. Cut 2 each black-foam bat wings (reversing one), triangular ears and white teeth. Cut 4 white-foam ghosts, varying shapes. Glue eyes to bat.

PAINT dimensional purple mouth on bat. (Practice using dimensional paints on scrap paper first.) Decorate front of wings with dimensional orange. Edge ghosts with neon. Let dry.

GLUE teeth and ears to bat with glue gun. Glue wings to back. Let dry. Push bat onto dowel top; glue. Cut four 13" wires. Coil each around a pencil; remove and stretch slightly. Bend and glue one end to back of ghost. Poke and glue other end into back of pumpkin, arranging ghosts to hover around pumpkins.

HALLOWEEN MOBILE

Fun Foam: white and black
Dimensional paints (we used orange, white,
    green and black Tulip Slick)
Tacky glue (we used Aleene's Fast Grab)
Pinking shears
White fabric scrap
Orange plastic plates
Black permanent marker
Hole punch
Black yarn
12" blue needlepoint hoop

USING photo, right, as guide, cut out bat and ghost shapes from craft foam. Decorate with dimensional paint; let dry.

GLUE strips of white fabric, cut with pinking shears, to bottom of ghost.

CUT edge off each plastic plate to leave flat middle. Use black marker to draw face and border on plate.

PUNCH hole at top of bat, ghost and pumpkin.

THREAD black yarn through and tie to needlepoint hoop. To hang hoop, cut three 18" lengths of yarn.

TIE all three together at one end. Tie other ends at equal distances around hoop.

LANTERNS (E)

FOR EACH ONE

Tin can
Clamp
Hammer and nail
Sandpaper
Metal primer
Acrylic paints: orange and black
Several yds of 18–20-gauge black annealed
    stovepipe wire
Tacky glue (we used Aleene's Original)
Votive candle

CLAMP can to table and poke holes for handle on opposite sides ½" below top with hammer and nail.

SAND, PRIME, THEN PAINT outside of can orange.

PENCIL outline of a jack-o'-lantern face on front and punch holes along outlines. Paint face black. Let dry.

WIND 27" wire around a bunch of pencils or a thick dowel; remove and fasten ends in holes. Glue votive in place. When candle is lit, bend handle away so it doesn't heat up.

NEVER leave lit candles unattended.

WREATH ❶

Two 12" squares corrugated or other sturdy
   cardboard
Drawing compass
Low-temp glue gun
1 yd 14-gauge wire
Pliers
Duct tape
12 tennis balls
Acrylic paints (we used Plaid FolkArt Green,
   Lavender, Spring White and Apple Barrel Orange)
Scrap of black fabric
1 each 9" x 12" lavender, green, orange and
   black felt sheets
Fabric glue
Six ³⁄₈" orange buttons
Lavender and black yarn
Scraps of black net (optional)
12" of ¹⁄₈" black dotted ribbon

DRAW a 9½"-diam circle on cardboard and another 1" larger around it; cut 2 for 1"-wide, 11½"-diam wreath. Glue wreaths back to back with glue gun. Bend wire circle with pliers to support center back of wreath; interlock ends; tape to back of wreath.

PAINT 3 balls of each color (2 coats). Hot-glue balls to wreath, alternating colors.

CHARACTERS (MAKE 3 EACH): Draw patterns for faces, following photo for ideas.

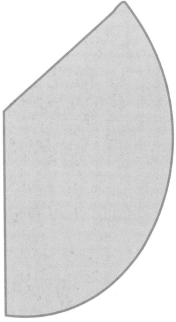

PUMPKIN: Cut face from black fabric; glue to orange ball. From short end, roll 1" x 8" green felt tightly for stem; glue side closed with fabric glue. Glue end to pumpkin.

WITCH: Trace witch's hat peak shape, left. Glue button eyes and small (½" x ¾") triangular orange-felt nose to green ball. Draw zigzag mouth with black paint. Glue on lavender-yarn hair. Cut black felt peak from pattern and 3"-diam black-felt circle for brim; roll and glue peak; glue to brim. Add optional net bow. Glue to head.

GHOUL: Cut white-fabric eyes and nose; add black lines for teeth. Roll a 1" x 4" strip of green felt tightly for nose. Glue to lavender ball. Add black-yarn hair. For stovepipe hat, roll 1" x 11" orange felt; glue side closed; glue bottom to center of a 2"-diam orange felt circle for brim.

GHOST: Glue on black-fabric features. Add white eye dots. For top hat, roll ¾" x 11" lavender felt; glue side closed; glue to 1½"-diam lavender circle for brim. Add ribbon band.

HALLOWEEN WREATH Ⓔ

15"–17" grapevine wreath
Dry twigs
Wired candy corn, spiders, skeletons, fans of orange craft paper
Spool of fishing line
Artificial web
Small skeleton

INSERT dry twigs in a vine wreath.

TIE on wired candy corn, spiders, skeletons, fans of orange craft paper, etc. with fishing line.

DRAPE artificial web over wreath.

TIE on skeleton at bottom of wreath.

PUMPKIN GARLAND Ⓘ

9 small (3") wooden pumpkin cutouts
Drill with ¼" bit
Sandpaper
Acrylic paints (we used Plaid FolkArt Pure Orange, Calico Red, Teddy Bear Tan, Teddy Bear Brown, Licorice and Warm White)
Clean rag
Small paintbrushes
Black fine-point permanent marker
Twine or paper twine in desired length of garland
Raffia
Wired candy corn

DRILL hole into each pumpkin below stem. Sand edges.

RUB orange paint into wood with rag. Add dabs of red at edges. Paint stems tan with brown accents. Let dry.

OUTLINE face with marker. Fill in with Licorice paint. Add white dot to eyes.

SAND edges of pumpkin randomly to remove some paint.

THREAD pumpkins on string. Tie in place facing forward, evenly spaced, with raffia. Attach candy corn.

COSTUMES D

Note for all costumes (including those on following pages): these costumes are sized to fit a child about six to ten years old. Adjust measurements as needed to fit your child.

Felt or fabric: 1 yd or less for cape or tunic, 24" x 14" for any helmet

1 yd of ½"–1"-wide ribbon or elastic 2" longer than neck circumference for capes

Hook-and-loop fastener for helmets

Extra material and thread or fabric glue (or paper-backed fusible web) for appliquéd designs (see individual patterns)

Assorted trims (see individual costume instructions)

Coordinating sweatshirts and pants will help complete these simple costumes

BASIC CAPE: Use fabric widthwise or lengthwise; cut as needed. Finish sides and bottom by turning under ¼", then 1"; stitch (felt edges don't have to be finished). Make a casing at top by turning under ¼", then a flap ½" wider than the ribbon or elastic; stitch along first fold. Guide ribbon or elastic through casing with a large safety pin. Stitch ribbon at center back so it doesn't slip out, or stitch ends of elastic in place and add hook-and-loop fastener at neck.

BASIC HELMET: Enlarge or copy pattern below (see *How to Enlarge Patterns,* page 144), and cut 2 from fabric. With right sides together, ¼" seam allowance, stitch top and back seam. Check fit on head and make any adjustments. Turn under edges ¼" twice (except on felt); topstitch. Sew hook-and-loop fastener at front neck.

COW OR DOG: 1. Stitch a cape and hood from black-and-white-spotted cotton knit. **2.** Cut black felt rounded ears approximately 3½" wide x 4" long and pink-felt inner ears ¾" smaller on 3 upper sides. Sew or glue inner to outer ears matching lower edges. Sew one to each side of hood.

JESTER: 1. Fold black felt in half over shoulders to make a tunic. Cut centered 9"-wide shallow neckline, or size to slip over head. **2.** Cut about fifty 2¾" or so felt squares for Harlequin design (if using iron-on fusing material, attach before cutting). Arrange squares in rows with points touching and sew, iron or glue on. **3.** Hat: Cut six 7½" x 12" felt rectangles desired colors. Pin in pairs, alternating colors as you like. Mark lower edge of pairs 4½" from left-hand corner; cut curve from mark to upper right corner. With right sides together, ¼" seam allowance, seam pairs on curved and long straight edges. Then pin 7" edge of 1 piece on 1 pair to matching edge of 1 piece on next pair; repeat around to form hat; stitch, leaving 1 seam open. Cut a 2"-wide band to fit around head, plus ¼". Stitch to bottom, easing in edge of hat. Stitch last seam. Turn. Sew a bell to each point.

PUMPKIN: 1. Cut orange felt cape and hood. Stitch elastic in casing at neck. **2.** Cut black-felt triangles with 6" sides for pumpkin's eyes and nose, and a 20"-wide mouth. Sew, glue or fuse to back of cape. **3.** Cut scalloped edges on three 9" x 12" pieces of green felt for leaves. Hand-sew, overlapped and gathered, to neck for collar. **4.** Cut a few large green leaf shapes and sew to hood. Cut a 2" x 7" strip for stem. Fold in half and sew long sides closed; pad with fiberfill; sew to crown of hood. **5.** Tack 1"-wide, long green felt ties to neck.

BUMBLEBEE: 1. Stitch a yellow-and-black-striped tunic (see Jester, Step 1) and black hood. **2.** Tie or glue center of a black chenille stem to top of a black headband; fold ends up for feelers; tip with glitter pompoms. **3.** Wings: Form four 10"-diam ovals each from 32" white wires. Wrap tulle over each oval and secure smoothly at one edge. Tack 2 ovals side by side to form each wing. Cut two 2" x 8" strips of white felt or fabric. Sew 2" of wing joinings between them at each end. Sew on elastic loops to fit around shoulders.

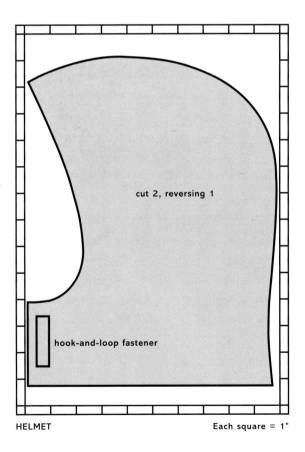

cut 2, reversing 1

hook-and-loop fastener

HELMET

Each square = 1"

SNAKE COSTUME Ⓓ

1½ yds of tube green knit neck ribbing
Green and black thread
Green ribbed adult sock
1 each red and white chenille stems
    (for tongue and fangs)
Low-temp glue gun
2 black ⅝" Velcro Sticky-Back coins
Two 22 mm movable eyes
16 oz of fiberfill stuffing
1 pkg green and 1 assorted colors of ¾" Paillette
    Sequins (we used Sulyn Inc.)
Small prescription bottle with lid and seed beads
    or beans for rattle
Yellow ribbed adult sock
Four 9" x 12" yellow felt sheets
Pinking shears
6" of ¼"-wide elastic
¼ yd of black 1½"-wide Velcro Brand Sew-On Hook
    and Loop Fastener
Green baseball cap, sweatshirt and pants

NOTE: Snake is about 3 yds long. Read instructions and determine appropriate length for your child.

CUT knit tube in half lengthwise. Fold each strip in half lengthwise, wrong side out. With ¼" seam allowance, stitch long edges closed, tapering one slightly, to have 2 tubes.

STUFF tubes. Hand-sew matching ends together to have 3-yds-long snake.

STUFF green sock for head. Bend red chenille stem to form forked tongue. Glue bottom of heel to foot to form mouth, inserting tongue (see photo).

STICK Velcro coins to front for nostrils. Glue eyes to head. Form fangs from white chenille stem; glue to mouth under nose.

HAND-SEW cuff of sock over thick end of tube, stuffing as needed.

GLUE green sequins along back of snake's head.

FILL prescription bottle with beads or beans to make rattle. Place in yellow-sock foot; stuff foot lightly, surrounding bottle. Flatten and stitch 3 or 4 sections across foot, securing bottle. Hand-sew cuff over narrow end of tube.

TRACE diamond patterns below. Cut 16 large and 9 small from felt with pinking shears. Glue tip to tip along back of snake, with smaller ones toward tail. Glue a sequin at each side of each juncture.

STITCH elastic loop to tail for wristband.

SEW hook side of Velcro along top and back of baseball cap; sew loop side to snake belly just below head. Adhere snake to cap.

TO WEAR: Place cap on child's head. Wrap snake around shoulders, then around trunk and slip elastic loop on child's wrist to hold up tail.

SPIDER COSTUME  D

1²/₃ yds of thermal fleece with silver face
Low-temp glue gun
¼ yd of white ¾"-wide Velcro Brand Sew-On Hook
*   and Loop Fastener*
2" plastic-foam ball
Two 36 mm movable eyes
¼ yd of shiny purple fabric
Basketball to prop helmet while gluing
Scrap of Fun Foam
Two 12" chenille stems
Straight pins
3 yds of 3¼"-wide sequin-band ribbon (in fabric/
*   crafts stores; leftover from sequin cutting)*
16 oz of fiberfill stuffing
3 yds of silver elastic cord
3 pairs inexpensive purple (or other color) tights
*   for legs*

BASIC HELMET: Enlarge pattern, page 22 (see *How to Enlarge Patterns,* page 144). Cut from fleece. Stitch top/back seam with right sides together, ¼" seam allowance. Glue darts to fit child. Sew on Velcro for neck closure.

CUT plastic-foam ball in half for eyes. Glue movable eyes to curved side. Trace eyelash pattern, right. Cut 2 sets from Fun Foam and glue to back of ball, placing helmet on basketball to work. Glue 3"-diam circle of shiny purple fabric each side of helmet seam near front. Glue eyes to circles. Form antennae from chenille stems and glue to top seam.

CUT 4 ovals (about 19" x 21") from fleece for back and front of body (you can round off a rectangle or trace an oval tub). Pin ovals together in pairs with silver sides out. Topstitch close to outer edges.

TOPSTITCH 2–3 strips of sequin band (crossed at center) to outer surface of each oval. Glue 3" circles of shiny fabric in spaces on back if you like.

CUT 2 silver shoulder straps about 8" long. Stitch to top of back piece. Stitch one to front piece. Attach Velcro to close other strap at front.

STUFF legs of tights with fiberfill; cut off at 18" or desired length for spider's legs. Pin and stitch top of 3 legs each under long sides of back oval. Starting with rear leg on each side, tie cord from leg to leg near ends, leaving about 2" cord between legs. At front, tie cord in a loop to fit child's wrist, so legs move when child moves arms.

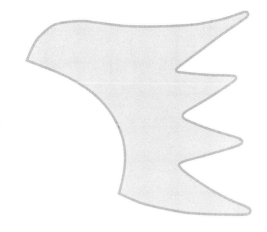

DRAGON COSTUME ⒟

1¼ yds of red knit sequined fabric
Low-temp glue gun
1 yd of red or black ¾"-wide Velcro Brand Sew-On
    Hook and Loop Fastener
3" plastic-foam ball
Two 36 mm movable eyes
3 sheets of red Fun Foam (Westrim)
12 red 12" wired chenille stems
Basketball to prop helmet while gluing
Red sweatshirt and tights

ENLARGE helmet pattern, page 22 (see *How to Enlarge Patterns,* page 144).

FOLD sequined fabric in half with selvages matching. Cut tunic on fold and helmet (adding selvage to length) as shown in diagram. Trace saucer or jar lid to cut 4" diam circle at center of fold on tunic for neck, then make a 4" slit down from neck on back.

STITCH helmet top/back seam with right sides together, ¼" seam allowance.

FIT and adjust pieces to child, gluing darts. Sew on 2" strips of Velcro to close helmet and sides of tunic at waist, ½" strip to close back neck.

EYES: Cut plastic-foam ball in half. Glue eye to curved side of each half. Cover back half of eye with selvage fabric for eyelid. Trace eyelash pattern printed over text and cut 2 from Fun Foam. Glue to bottom of eyes protruding around lid.

ARMS: Cut two 5" x 12" Fun Foam strips. Cut a row of points at one end. Cover outside with sequined fabric. Cut a 10" strip Velcro. Separate strip and glue or staple 5" of one half across center of wrong side of "arm," with 5" extending to one side. Press on Velcro mate with 5" excess facing opposite direction, so strips can reattach when circled around arm.

SCALES: Cut three 5" x 5" Fun Foam triangles on a ½" strip shaped according to back of helmet pattern (see diagram, right). Then cut rows of triangles along remaining Fun Foam for tail. Glue chenille stems along sides of ½" lower edges to stabilize strips. Glue all triangles together to form one strip.

ASSEMBLY: Place helmet on basketball. Glue eyes in place, holding until secure. Glue curved scales along helmet seam, pinching up fabric if necessary. Let remaining scales hang free for tail. Wear over red sweatshirt and tights.

PRINCESS COSTUME ⓘ

Satiny fabric
Princess costume pattern (we used McCall's #5207)
Lace or braid
Cardboard
Fabric glue
Silk scarf or other sheer fabric

USE satiny fabric and a princess costume pattern, or stitch a simple T-shaped tunic to fit your child. Trim with lace or braid.

MAKE cone-shaped hat as directed in your pattern, or roll a cardboard cone and glue fabric over it.

GLUE edge of a silk scarf or sheer fabric along back seam of hat as a streamer.

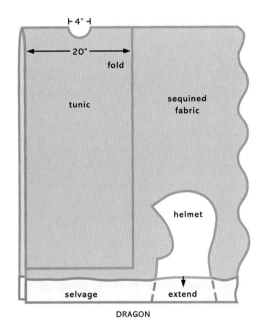

⊢ 4" ⊣

20"

fold

tunic

sequined
fabric

helmet

selvage   extend

DRAGON

5½"

5"

½"

Scales:
Shape curve
from helmet
pattern.

DRAGON SCALES

MONSTER COSTUME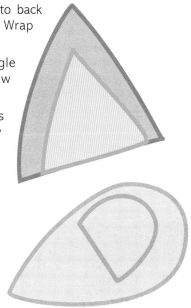

Purple sweatsuit
Raglan shoulder pads
Safety pins
Scraps of fabric and felt
8", 14" and 18" gray zippers
Low-temp glue gun
Velcro coins
No-Sew glue (we used Aleene's)
Bandages
Three 9" x 12" felt sheets: 2 black, 1 red
Glitter dimensional paint (we used Plaid Night Star)
Tissue paper

SUIT: Pin pads into sweatshirt shoulders. Cut felt and fabric patches. Open zippers; glue a thin strip of red felt to backs to show between teeth. Glue Velcro coins to ends of 14" and 8" zippers to fasten as collar and bracelet. With No-Sew glue, place 18" zipper on pant leg and patches on suit. Add safety pins and bandages all over.

HAIR: With right sides of black felt together, stitch 9" sides and 12" top closed. To box corners, refold to have top and side seams matching. Stitch across corners 1½" from points. Trim. Turn right side out. Pin pleats at back to fit. Cut bangs. Stripe each with glitter. Add pins and patches. Stuff lightly with tissue.

SCAREDY CAT COSTUME

Steel gray, red and pink felt
No-Sew glue (we used Aleene's)
Glitter dimensional paint (we used Plaid Night Star)
Plastic headband
Low-temp glue gun
Gray gloves
Pink feather boa
Gray sweatsuit
25 mm jingle bell
1" x 18" yellow ribbon
Lensless cat-eye shaped glasses
For optional mouse: light-gray felt; 7 mm pink pompom; two 7 mm movable eyes; black chenille stem; small yellow bow; fiberfill stuffing

ENLARGE mouse and ear patterns, right (see *How to Enlarge Patterns*, page 144).

EARS: Cut 2 steel-gray and 2 pink, reversing 1 each. Glue in pairs. Outline with glitter paint. Let dry. Glue to headband with glue gun.

CLAWS: Cut red pointed fingernails; glue to glove tips.

TAIL: Pin end of boa to back of pants near waist. Wrap around arm or body.

COLLAR: Thread jingle bell through yellow ribbon; tie in back.

MOUSE: Cut 2 bodies and ears from light-gray felt, reversing 1 each. Stitch bodies with ¼" seam, leaving opening at bottom. Clip seam allowance. Turn right side out. Stuff; sew closed. Fold and glue pleat in ears; glue to head. Glue on eyes and pompom nose. Sew dental floss or thread through snout for whiskers. Glue on 6" chenille "tail." Glue bow to tail. Glue mouse to top of headband.

JACK-O'-LANTERN COSTUME

9" x 12" yellow felt sheet
No-Sew glue (we used Aleene's)
Dimensional paint (we used Plaid Orange-Yellow Neon)
Orange sweatshirt and red or orange sweatpants
Green gloves
Paintbrushes
13¼"-diam circle of orange felt or orange beret
3" x 9" green felt sheet
Brown or white paper
Acrylic paints (we used Plaid Apple Barrel, Cardinal Crimson, Harvest Orange, Christmas Green, Bright Yellow)

CUT yellow eyes, nose and mouth from yellow felt.

GLUE to front of sweatshirt. Outline with dimensional paint. Let dry.

LID HAT: Use beret, or baste along edge of orange felt circle with dental floss or strong thread; pull to gather; tie off.

ROLL green felt stem; glue closed and to hat. Cut paper leaves; paint in fall colors. Pin or glue to costume.

MA AND PA ❶ SCARECROW

Lumber (supplier may cut): two 24" 4 x 4s for bodies,
*   22" 1 x 3 for arms and 12" 2 x 12 for base*
Sandpaper
Acrylic paints (we used Aleene's Premium-Coat
*   Acrylic in Burgundy, Ivory, Black, Blush, Dusty*
*   Blue, Dusty Mauve and Yellow Ochre)*
1", ³⁄₈" flat and liner paintbrushes
Transfer paper
¹⁄₄ yd of burlap
Drawing compass
³⁄₄ yd of gold jumbo rickrack
Scrap of gold felt
Raffia
Low-temp glue gun
Twelve 2" nails
Strong brewed tea
¹⁄₂ yd of ⁵⁄₈" lace trim
6" lace doily

SAND wood; wipe with damp cloth.

BASE: Paint upper surface of base piece burgundy for Ma, dusty blue for Pa. When dry, with tip of brush handle dot with ivory. Paint sides ivory. When dry, pencil then paint black triangles for Ma and squares for Pa.

HEAD: Mark upper 4¹⁄₄" of body for head and 8" below that for blouse or shirt. Paint head blush. Trace face, opposite; transfer to wood. Paint nose burgundy, cheeks mauve and eyes black. When dry, paint black mouth with liner brush, dot ivory highlight on eye.

BLOUSE/SHIRT: Paint Ma's blouse and arms burgundy; dot with ivory when dry. Paint Pa's shirt and arms ivory. When dry, paint water-thinned blue grid with ³⁄₈" brush for gingham. Let dry. Paint intersections of grid full-strength blue.

SKIRT/PANTS: Paint Ma's skirt ivory-and-burgundy gingham, Pa's overalls blue, buttons black and patches as shown.

HAT: Cut burlap half-circle with 8" radius. Lap sides to form cone; glue. Fold up front brim; glue. Glue rickrack along Ma's brim; felt heart to Pa's. Tie 8"-long bundle of raffia; cut hole in top of hat and glue raffia up through hole.

FINISHING: Glue and nail figures to center of bases. Attach arms to back with 2 nails. To antique lace, dip pieces in strong tea. Let dry. Cut doily in half; hot-glue cut edges around Ma's neck. Tie lace around waist. Glue hats to heads.

SCARECROW BASKET

7½" x 27" red checked fabric
Fiberfill stuffing
Raffia
Low-temp glue gun
7"-diam basket
14" square muslin
4" plastic-foam ball (optional)
Acrylic paints (we used Aleene's Premium-Coat in
    Dusty Mauve, Black, Ivory, Burgundy)
Small round and flat paintbrushes
Black fine-point permanent marker
Needle and thread
¼ yd or 9" x 20" burlap
Drawing compass
Scrap of red felt
¾" flat button
Small unpainted wooden bird

ARMS: Turn under ¼" on short edges of checked fabric; topstitch. Fold lengthwise, wrong side out; stitch long edge with ¼" seam. Turn right side out; stuff.

HANDS: Cut two 8"-long bunches of raffia; fold each in half and tie with raffia near fold. Hot-glue folded ends into ends of arms. Tie raffia around sleeves at wrists. Sew arms to outer top edge of basket.

HEAD: Trace face, right, on center of muslin square. Paint nose mauve with burgundy shading. Dab on water-thinned mauve cheeks. Draw mouth and outline eyes and nose with marker, adding short "stitch" lines as in photo. Paint eyes black. When dry, dot 2 ivory highlights on each eye with brush handle. Wrap muslin around plastic-foam ball (or stuff firmly); secure on back with a rubber band. Trim excess.

BIRD: Paint black with yellow beak. Add white dots.

COLLAR: Hand-sew running stitches ½" from 1 long edge of 2½" x 20" burlap; pull thread to gather; fasten. Glue raffia scraps under gathered edge; glue collar under head.

HAT: Cut burlap half-circle with 6" radius. Glue sides closed. Fold up brim at front; glue. Cut red felt moon. Glue moon to brim, button to moon. Cut hole at top and glue in some raffia.

GLUE OR SEW head to arms off center. Glue hat to head and bird to basket rim.

LITTLE MUMMIES ⓔ

FOR EACH ONE

One ⅞" x 6" and four ⅜" x 4½" craft sticks
Craft knife
Tacky glue
Gauze
Scraps of Fun Foam
Two 5 mm movable eyes

SCORE line across large craft stick 3" from one end; snap off excess. Glue thin craft stick across back 1" below curved end for arms; glue legs below arms. Let dry.

CUT long ½"-wide strips of gauze. Starting at top, wrap body and one leg with one strip; glue ends to back. Wrap arms and remaining leg.

CUT ¼" x ½" foam strip; glue across middle of head. Glue eyes to strip.

MUMMY ⓘ

¼" plywood 14" x 24" (body), 15" x 24" (cat and bat)
Saber saw
1" and 1½" drywall screws
Pine lumber: 30", 10" and two 24" 1 x 6; 24" and
*   13" 1 x 8; two 5½" 2 x 4*
White wood primer
Flat brush, ¼" stencil brush, round brush
Glow-in-the-Dark paint (we used Delta Ceramcoat
*   Warm Green, Atomic Orange, Clear Glow)*
2"-wide long strips of white fabric (old sheet)
Low-temp glue gun
Black acrylic paint
1½" hinge for brace

CUT head in plywood with saber saw and assemble wood frame with screws, following diagram, below. Cut 3" circular nose and 3" x 5" hands from 10" length of 1 x 6 pine; indent fingers. Cut triangular brace for back from 13" 1 x 8; cut 85-degree angle in end to slant edge.

SCREW nose on. Add 2 x 4 feet at front.

PRIME face, feet, hands and sign. Let dry. Paint body parts green, sign orange.

TEAR long 1½"-wide strips of cloth. Starting at top, wind around frame, leaving face exposed. Glue as needed to prevent shifting; tie on strips as you go.

BRUSH clear glow over fabric. Paint black letters on sign with stencil brush. Paint eyes and finger lines. Screw hands and sign on.

ATTACH brace with hinge. Add stakes at bottom for outdoor use.

CAT AND BAT: Enlarge patterns, opposite (see *How to Enlarge Patterns*, page 144). Cut from wood adding 3" points as stakes to cat's legs. Paint. Wrap with ½"-wide strips of cloth. Screw bat to back of mummy's arm. Insert cat in ground.

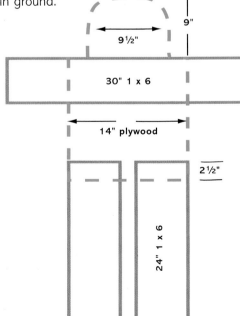

Each square = 4"

PLASTISPOOKS

FOR EACH ONE

White plastic spoon
Black fine-point permanent marker or Apple Barrel
   Indoor/Outdoor Acrylic Enamel and small
   paintbrush
4 white plastic forks
White Fun Foam
Low-temp glue gun
Spring-clip clothespins
White chenille stem

DRAW face on back of spoon bowl and dots along handle for spine with marker or paint, following photo. Draw long lines for bones on front of fork handles and dots for short bones on tines.

CUT ovals for shoulders and hips from foam or felt. Center across top and bottom on back of spoon handle; glue and clamp with clothespin until dry.

GLUE arms to shoulders and legs to hips at front; clamp with clothespins.

WIND chenille loosely around spine for rib cage; glue ends to back of shoulders and hips.

POMPOM SKELETON

Pompoms: 1 white 1", 23 white ³⁄₄", 6 black ¹⁄₄"
Low-temp glue gun or tacky glue
Scraps of white Fun Foam
Large needle
18" elastic cord

GLUE ³⁄₄" pompom to 1" head for neck, 8 in triangle for body, 3 each for arms and legs, and 1 each for feet. Glue on black pompom eyes, nose and mouth.

CUT hands and toe section of feet from foam. Glue in place. Bring needle threaded with elastic up through back of head. Tie loop for hanger.

GOURD-O

*Clean orange plastic laundry detergent container
  with green cap (Tide, for example), or paint cap
  with a paint for plastic*
Craft knife, tracing paper, pencil
Scraps of cotton print fabric
1 each 9" x 12" yellow and green felt sheets
Tacky glue (we used Aleene's Quick Dry)
2 green chenille stems

REMOVE labels from container. In handle finger space, measure down ½" from top and draw a line around container (not handle); cut carefully along line with craft knife.

CUT 2"-diam circles for eyes, 2" triangle for nose and wide smiling mouth from fabrics. From felt, cut two 1½" yellow circles and two ¾" green circles for eyes, 1" yellow triangle for nose and a row of yellow teeth. Apply to front of container layered as in photo, using a generous amount of glue. Let dry.

TRACE half-leaf pattern printed over text. Cut from green felt, placing dashed line on fold. Cut one 8" and two 2" lengths from one chenille stem. Glue to back of leaf as stem and veins. Let dry. Coil the other chenille stem around your finger. Bend and connect ends of stems. Remove container cap; wrap stem smoothly around top of container and screw cap on firmly to secure leaf.

BOTTLE GHOSTS

FOR EACH ONE

Glass or plastic bottle
Beans or rice
Large white terry-lined tube socks
Low-temp glue gun
Scraps of black felt, colored felt, fabrics
18-gauge wire as needed; wire snips
Black dimensional paint
Fabric glue (optional)

WASH and dry bottle; remove label. Pour in enough beans to weight. Re-cap.

PULL inside-out sock down over bottle, leaving 3" loose at top. Trim bottom; glue around bottle with glue gun. Twist top to point; glue.

CUT 4 triangular arms desired size. Form wire triangles to stiffen arms. Glue inside; glue arms to ghost. Cut and glue on black features, colored patches, bows. Paint black stitches around patches. Make felt or fabric bag or sign for ghost to carry. Glue on (with fabric glue) or attach with wire or toothpick.

TREAT BAGS ❶

9" x 12" sheet of red, peacock or yellow
   felt for each bag
Tacky glue
Two 20 mm movable eyes for each bag
Matching thread
Appliqués:
Cat: Four 9" x 12" felt sheets: 2 black,
   1 each yellow and baby pink; scrap white
   Dimensional paints (we used Plaid Night Star
   Glitter and Teal Shiny)
   Dental floss; needle
Monster: Five 9" x 12" felt sheets: 2 lime,
   3 yellow, scraps of orchid and steel gray
   Dimensional paints (we used Plaid Hot
   Green Neon and Night Star Glitter)
Jack-o'-Lantern: Four 9" x 12" felt sheets:
   2 orange, 1 each lime and yellow
   Dimensional paints (we used Plaid Orange-Yellow
   Neon and Hot Green Neon)

ENLARGE patterns below (see *How to Enlarge Patterns*, page 144). Cut from felt, adding ¼" underlap where pieces butt. Glue to one bag piece, as below.

CAT: Glue head to bag piece, details to head and yellow moon across top. With teal paint, print "TREATS" across moon and outline eyes. Border felt shapes with glitter paint. Let dry. From back, thread dental-floss whiskers through cheeks; knot on front; trim to 5". Dot knots with glitter.

MONSTER: Glue shoulders, then head, to bag piece, features to face, lids over movable eyes. Cut bangs; add hair. Tuck bolts under jaw. Outline green pieces with green paint, others with glitter.

JACK-O'-LANTERN: Glue whole pumpkin to bag. Cut second layer for sections 2 and 4; glue on. Add face, leaves and stem. Paint orange outline on sections and face, green veins on leaves and stripe on stem.

FINISHING: Glue eyes on each bag. Pin second felt sheet to back, right side out. Topstitch sides and bottom ⅛" from edge. For handles, cut two 4" x 12" strips from third felt piece. Fold each in half lengthwise, wrong side out; stitch long edges closed. Turn right side out. Center 1" ends of 1 each at top over back and front of seams; stitch.

Each square = 2"

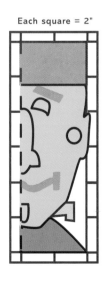

BEJEWELED AND CAT BAGS (E)

Lunch-size natural and black paper bags
Hole punch
Craft jewels
Gemstone glue
Construction paper remnants
Raffia or ribbon; tweezers (optional)

BEJEWELED BAG: From the top of a paper bag, cut 2" slits down all four corners. Fold side flaps inside bag. Trim corners off top of bag and punch holes along edge. To make handle, cut semicircle out of bag ½" from top.

DECORATE with small craft jewels. Lightly outline Halloween design onto front of bag with pencil. Glue jewels along outline. (A pair of tweezers is helpful.) Add raffia or ribbon tie.

CAT BAGS: With black paper bag folded flat, cut out ears from top. Cut inside ear shape from construction paper. Glue on jewel eyes and triangle ears. Tie several strands of raffia together to make whiskers and glue to face.

LOOT BAG (E)

Bright orange posterboard
Drawing compass
Black construction paper
Lunch-size brown paper bag
Tacky glue (we used Aleene's Original)
Hole punch
½ yd of narrow raffia or ribbon

DRAW two 8" circles on posterboard; cut out. Draw scary cat shape on black paper, using photo above as guide.

CUT bag to 6" high.

GLUE circles to front and back of bag.

MAKE holes at center top of each circle. Tie ribbon to holes to make handle.

BOUNCING GHOSTS

Assorted solid-color socks
Iron-on paper-backed fusible web
Scraps of black cotton fabric
Fiberfill stuffing
Scraps of colored and black Fun Foam for hats
Tacky glue (we used Aleene's Quick Dry)
Drawing compass
15" round black elastic or beading cord for each
Darning needle at least 2" long for elastic

CUT off sock cuff about 3" above heel to use foot as ghost. Cut jagged edge.

IRON web to wrong side of black fabric, leaving paper backing on. Draw ghostly eyes, nose and mouth on backing. Cut out. Peel off paper. Iron pieces onto sock with toe end as top. Stuff foot leaving heel unstuffed.

CUT a 2¾"-diam circle of Fun Foam for hat brim. Cut 1½" x 6" strip of foam for hat side. Lap and glue ends of strip to make a 1½"-diam tube. Trace one end and cut circular foam top. Glue to hat. Glue brim, centered, to other end.

THREAD elastic in needle; knot end. Insert needle into back of ghost about ½" below top, then out through center top, through center of hat brim and top of hat. Cut elastic, leaving at least 12" end for bouncing or hanging. Glue hat to head.

GHOSTLY GOURDS

3 dry oblong gourds
Acrylic paints: white and black
Flat and fine round paintbrushes
Scrap fabrics
Pinking shears
Low-temp glue gun
¼"-wide elastic
Optional: wood for base, colored paints

PAINT gourds several coats of white until covered, letting dry after each coat.

PAINT ghostly face in black. Let dry.

CUT ½"-wide strip of fabric to fit around Dad's neck using pinking shears. Cut shape for long necktie twice desired length; knot around center of strip. Glue strip around ghost. Tie or shape bow tie. Glue to a strip of ¼"-wide elastic to make a circle to fit boy. Place around neck. Tie bow around gourd stem for Mom, or glue a bow to top.

Optional: **PAINT** square of wood for base. Let dry. Glue ghost on top.

THREE HAPPY GHOSTS Ⓔ

Three 8" white paper lanterns
Acrylic paints: pink and black
Six ¼" red pompoms
¼ yd of white cotton fabric
Tacky glue (we used Aleene's Original)
Fishing line

PAINT pink cheeks and big, black ghostly mouths on each lantern.

GLUE pompom eyes to each face.

CUT fabric into long jagged strips. Glue strips behind each lantern.

GLUE lantern frames together. Thread fishing line through top lantern for hanging.

GHOST BOWL Ⓔ

Large glass bowl
Glass cleaner or rubbing alcohol
Masking tape
Rubber gloves and goggles (for Armour Etch)
Glass etching cream (Armour Etch) or etch-like paint
   (Delta PermEnamel White Frost)
Paintbrush

WASH and dry bowl. Clean with glass cleanser or alcohol to remove any grease.

SKETCH paper patterns for ghosts. Cut out and tape inside bowl facing out.

BRUSH cream or paint onto outside of bowl over pattern, following manufacturer's instructions for handling.

BANDANNA GHOSTS ⓔ

FOR EACH ONE

Colored bandanna
String
2 chenille stems
Tacky glue (we used Aleene's Fast Grab)
Orange yarn
Scraps of black felt or Fun Foam
Two 4 mm movable eyes

BUNCH sheet of paper into ball. Place in middle of bandanna; tie with string to make head.

TWIST 2 chenille stems together. Bend in middle and insert about 1" into the inside of ghost head where it is tied with string. Apply small amount of glue; let dry. Bend chenille stems out to form arm shapes.

KNOT yarn at one end several times. Glue to top of head; let dry.

CUT mouth from felt or foam; glue on head. Glue on movable eyes.

SCATTER PINS ⓔ

Scraps of balsa wood
Craft knife
Acrylic paints (we used FolkArt Pure Orange, Green,
  Lemon Custard, Spring White,
  Pure Black)
Small paintbrushes
Plain cut-wood letters
Fabri-tac fabric glue
Black fine-point
  permanent marker
Satin finish varnish
Pin backs

CUT shapes from balsa wood, using patterns, right; paint white, let dry, then paint colors.

GLUE letters to background. Add details with marker.

APPLY coat of varnish. Let dry. Glue on pin back.

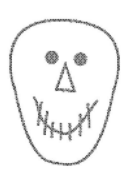

GHOST HEADBAND ⓔ

Plain or purple headband
Purple felt (if you use a plain headband)
Fabric glue
Sewing needle and purple thread (optional)
Scrap of white Fun Foam or felt
Black fine-point permanent marker

CUT felt slightly larger than headband.

COVER headband with felt. Glue or stitch underside.

CUT ghost from foam or felt; add features with marker.

GLUE ghost to side of headband.

GHOST PENDANT ⓔ

6"-diam circle white cotton fabric
Plaid Stiffy fabric stiffener
Foam paintbrush
Fabric glue
One 1" white pompom
Black fine-point permanent marker
1 yd of orange satin cord
Wire loop

COVER fabric circle with stiffener. Let dry. Glue pompom to center.

GATHER fabric all around pompom to form ghost. Trim edges for a ragged look. Add features with marker.

ADD wire loop and string with cord; tie around neck for desired length.

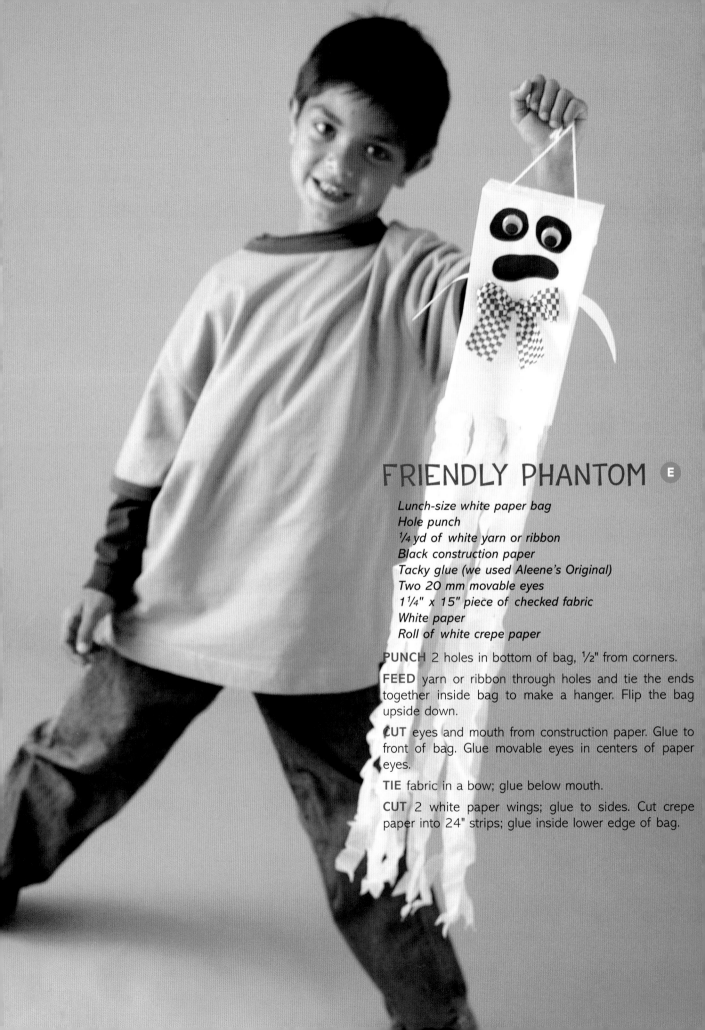

FRIENDLY PHANTOM (E)

Lunch-size white paper bag
Hole punch
¼ yd of white yarn or ribbon
Black construction paper
Tacky glue (we used Aleene's Original)
Two 20 mm movable eyes
1¼" x 15" piece of checked fabric
White paper
Roll of white crepe paper

PUNCH 2 holes in bottom of bag, ½" from corners.

FEED yarn or ribbon through holes and tie the ends together inside bag to make a hanger. Flip the bag upside down.

CUT eyes and mouth from construction paper. Glue to front of bag. Glue movable eyes in centers of paper eyes.

TIE fabric in a bow; glue below mouth.

CUT 2 white paper wings; glue to sides. Cut crepe paper into 24" strips; glue inside lower edge of bag.

SKELETONS ⓔ

FOR EACH ONE

8 plastic plates, all the same size
Hole punch
Raffia
Black fine-point permanent marker
Contrasting adhesive plastic (we used Con-Tact paper)
String or fishing line for hanging

DRAW on plates and cut out 1 each skull, chest and pelvis, 8 arm/leg bones, 2 each knees, hands and feet, following diagrams, below.

PUNCH holes at dots and tie bones together with raffia.

DRAW eyes, nose, ribs and square mouth on back of adhesive plastic. Cut out, dividing mouth with zigzag cut. Peel off backing and stick pieces to skeleton. Tie string or fishing line at top as hanger.

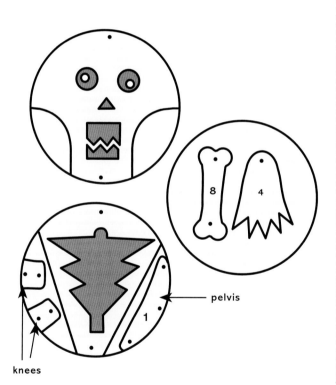

knees — pelvis

SPIDER BRACELET AND EARRINGS ⓔ

7" of beige Velcro sew-on tape
Fabric glue
Black covered wire
Eight 1" black pompoms: 6 for bracelet, 2 for earrings
Sixteen 4 mm movable eyes
Elastic thread
Earring backs

CUT 7" strip of loop (smooth) side of Velcro in half lengthwise. Cut a 1" piece of hook (rough) side in half lengthwise and glue to wrong side of loop piece.

CUT four 2" pieces of wire for each spider; glue under pompom; curl wire. Glue on eyes. Glue 6 spiders to Velcro.

THREAD short piece of elastic thread through bottom of each remaining spider. Tie or glue other end to earring backs.

SPIDERWEB CHOKER ⓔ

Fabric glue; craft knife; repositionable glue (such as Scotch Restickable glue stick)
Sheet of black Fun Foam
Scrap of purple Fun Foam
2 rhinestones
Black Velcro coin

COPY pattern, below, and enlarge to desired size (see *How to Enlarge Patterns*, page 144). Apply repositionable glue to back of pattern and lay on top of black foam.

CUT out pattern with craft knife through foam. Cut spider from foam scrap and glue on rhinestones for eyes.

GLUE Velcro coin to ends of choker.

fur by gluing edges and insert wire.) Poke 2 legs into Styrofoam ring at each side of body (snip hole in fur if necessary) and curve legs.

EYES: Glue pompoms to front.

HANGER: Attach hanging wire through fabric at center top if it will hold. Otherwise, poke hole through bowl at center, insert 4" stiff wire, bend wire ends to hold in place, and tie hanging wire or fishing line to loop.

SMALL SPIDER: GLUE fur over flower arranger. With fine wire, attach chenille to picks for legs and insert 2 on each side of body. Glue on pompom eyes. Attach wire to pick and insert at top for hanging.

WEB: TACK wire across porch opening, forming cross, then 8 pie sections, as shown in photo. Maintaining starting point at outlet, wind lights around wires or attach with electrical tape. String more lights crosswise from wire to wire, forming web.

SPOOKY SPIDERS

LARGE SPIDER
12" ring of plastic foam
12"-diam plastic bowl (like Tupperware) for body
Low-temp glue gun
36" square of black or gray fur fabric
*4 yds of black Jumbo Loopy Chenille (comes wired)
    for black spider legs*
Four 18" and one 4" stiff wire
Needlenose pliers
Two 2" pompoms
Wire or fishing line for hanging

SMALL SPIDER
*Styrofoam brand Flora Craft Flower Arranger
    for body*
10" square of fur
Fine wire for tying and hanging
Four 8" lengths of black Jumbo Loopy Chenille
5 short florist's picks
Two 1" pompoms

WEB
Tacks
Sturdy galvanized wire to span porch space
Strings of small outdoor lights

LARGE SPIDER: GLUE foam ring to top of bowl.

BODY: Cover bowl with fur fabric, concealing opening and cutting away excess on underside; glue fabric closed over opening.

LEGS: Bend ½" back at one end of each leg wire, using pliers. Wind chenille around each leg wire one way, then back to fill spaces. (Alternate leg method: Form tube of

SPIDERS

FOR EACH ONE
4"-diam straw hat
*Acrylic paints (we used FolkArt Licorice and
    Titanium White)*
Flat and round paintbrushes
FolkArt Outdoor Matte Sealer (optional)
4 each orange and black chenille stems
Scrap of orange Fun Foam
Two 15 mm movable eyes
Low-temp glue gun
Black yarn or string for hanging

PAINT hat crown 2 coats black, brim white. When dry, paint black web lines on brim. Let dry. Apply several coats of sealer if using outdoors.

CUT chenille stems in half. Twist black and orange in pairs to make 8 legs. Cut foam backing for eyes and mouth.

GLUE eyes to backing; glue eyes, mouth and legs to crown. Shape legs. Paint smile. Glue string to upper back.

WEB BAG ⓔ

2 each 9" x 12" pieces black and colored net
Black yarn
Tapestry needle
Black thread
Two 6 mm beads
Small plastic spider

WEAVE web, with yarn and needle, on 1 black net piece; begin and end all strands at the edge. Start with a spiral of about 3 rows, stopping at the center. Then weave a straight line out to the edge. Make 6 more lines out from center by weaving 1 strand in, then out in a different direction for each 2 lines.

SEW sides and bottom of black net pieces together, right sides out, with ¼" seam, catching in yarn ends. Stitch around top. Trim close to seam. Sew colored net lining in same way.

INSERT lining. Weave a yarn drawstring in and out through both layers 1½" from top. Add bead and knot to each end. Glue or sew spider to center of web.

MUFFIN-CUP SPIDERS ⓔ

FOR EACH ONE

Thin elastic cord
2 large colored paper baking cups
Tacky glue (we used Aleene's Fast Grab)
Sewing needle
4 chenille stems (or 8 for two-tone legs)
Low-temp glue gun
Two 10 mm movable eyes
2" length of ⅛"-wide red ribbon

TIE knot at one end of desired length of elastic cord. Use needle to pull cord through center of one baking cup. Apply thin line of glue along bottom outside edge of second cup. Then press second cup inside first, with cord threaded through center.

CUT chenille stems in half and glue to inside of each side of cup. (For two-tone legs: Twist 2 colors of chenille stems together, then glue to cup.) Use tacky glue to attach movable eyes and ribbon for mouth. Bend legs.

PUMPKIN DOORMAT  **E**

Transfer paper
At least three 6¼" x 5" rectangles of waxed
*   stencil paper or thin sturdy cardboard*
Craft knife
Natural bristle doormat (coir)
½"-wide masking tape
Acrylic paints (we used FolkArt Lavender,
*   Lemon Custard, Pure Orange, Buttercup,*
*   Green, Lipstick Red and Licorice)*
¾" stencil brushes

ENLARGE stencil pattern, below, 200% on a copier (see *How to Enlarge Patterns*, page 144) or draw a pumpkin in a 4" x 5¼" rectangle. Transfer image to center of 3 stencil rectangles. With craft knife, cut away background rectangle for stencil 1, pumpkin for stencil 2 and features for stencil 3, leaving outer stencil edges intact. (Note: Cut extras or plan to wash or let paint dry before changing color. Paint dries fast.)

PLAN colors and 3 rows of pumpkins spaced ½" apart across mat. Tape between rows.

STENCIL a few backgrounds (stencil 1), swirling brush to cover tips of mat bristles. Let dry. Stencil pumpkin in each space, with or without background. Let dry. Stencil faces. Let dry. Remove tape.

TOMBSTONE DOORMAT **I**

Tracing paper, transfer paper
Self-adhesive shelf liner (Con-Tact)
Craft knife or single-edge razor blade
Metal-edge ruler
½"-wide painter's tape or masking tape
Bristle or smooth doormat
½" straight pins
Acrylic paints (we used FolkArt Black and
*   Wicker White)*
Household sponge

PRINT "R.I.P." in large letters, about 8½" high, on tracing paper. With transfer paper under pattern, outline letters reversed on back of shelf liner.

CUT stencil for letters and periods on shelf liner, working on a hard surface with knife or blade. Guide straight cuts with ruler and cut shapes whole to use later as masks. Leave background intact. Repair any mistakes with tape.

CENTER stencil on doormat and secure edges with pins. Paint letters solid black with a piece of sponge. Remove stencil. Let dry.

MIX light gray paint from black and white. Pin cutouts over painted letters as masks. Sponge gray shadows to left of letters. Remove masks. Let dry.

TAPE outer edges of a ¼"-wide border stripe about 1" in from mat edge. Paint stripe black. Remove tape. Let dry. Cover stripe with tape. Paint gray shadows.

TOMBSTONE CHAIRS ⓔ

Matboard
Acrylic paints: black, white and gray
Sand
Chalk or charcoal sticks
Paintbrushes
String

CUT matboard to cover chair back. Mix a little sand into gray acrylic paint; paint both sides of matboard. Let dry.

DRAW gravestone images lightly on back with chalk or charcoal. Paint using mixtures of black and white acrylic. Let dry.

POKE holes for string; tie to chair.

GONE HAUNTING SIGN ⓔ

23" pine 1 x 6 or other wood
Hand saw
Drill with ¼" bit
Acrylic paints (we used FolkArt Wicker White, Green, Lavender, Tangerine, Black)
Sponge
Flat and round paintbrushes
1 yd of black wire

CUT jagged ends in wood with saw. Drill holes 5" from ends, ½" from top for wire.

PAINT board white. When dry, sponge on various colors. Let dry. Paint lettering with a shaky hand to give an eerie look.

INSERT wire hanger through holes. Curl ends on pencil.

SIGN OF THE TIMES ⓔ

Sheet of pine, plywood or heavy cardboard
Hand saw
8-ft pole or plank for post
Acrylic paints: white and black
Paintbrush

CUT pine, plywood or heavy cardboard for signs. Draw and cut out a skull and crossbones. Cut point in bottom of pole or plank for post.

PAINT dirty white backgrounds by painting signs white then dabbing with black paint. Rub off excess black paint while still wet. When dry, letter spooky destinations on signs and nail to post, pointing in different directions. Leave at least 15" at bottom of post.

PUSH post into ground or dig a hole and insert post.

SPOOKY SIGN ●

*¼" smooth exterior plywood 12" x 16"
  for sign and 14" x 18" for ghost*
Saber saw
Acrylic paints: white, orange, black and pink
Paintbrushes, stencil brush
Glue gun with wood-glue sticks
1⅝" x ¼" x 36" wood strip for stake

CUT plywood shapes from pattern, right (see *How to Enlarge Patterns*, page 144) with saber saw.

PAINT sign orange and ghost pieces white. When dry, stipple black around ghost edges and pink cheeks with paint very dry on stencil brush. Paint letters, lines and small ghost on sign.

HOT-GLUE ghost pieces to sign.

CUT a point at one end of stake. Glue 15" at other end to center back of sign.

Each square = 2"

WOODEN WITCH

Four 14" lengths of 1 x 4 pine and one 18" 1 x 4 or wider board for body
Scraps of ¼" plywood
Transfer paper
Saber saw
Acrylic paints: orange, green, black, white, yellow, dark pink and lavender
Paintbrushes
Wood glue
1½" and 1" nails
32" squares of black and red fabric
Fabric glue
Raffia
Duct tape
Broom
Wire or fishing line for hanging

ENLARGE or copy patterns, right (see *How to Enlarge Patterns*, page 144). Transfer to plywood and cut out with saber saw.

PAINT pieces.

GLUE and nail 14" 1 x 4s to front of 18" body for arms and legs (as on diagram, right). Glue and nail hands and feet to front of body outside broken lines on patterns. Attach head to other side of frame.

GLUE upper edge of black fabric along tops of arms; cut indented sides to shape dress; glue lower edge to legs. Knot top of red fabric for cape; cut fringe at bottom. Glue to neck. Add raffia hair.

TAPE broom across back. Attach witch to sheltered wall with nails and wire or fishing line.

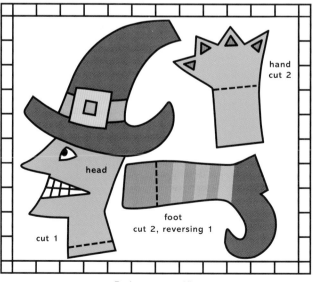

Each square = 2"

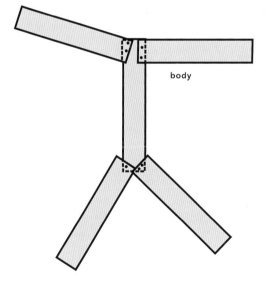

WICKED WITCH, CAT, ⒹCROWS AND GRAVES

60" x 48" sheet of smooth exterior ¼" plywood
17" x 23" scrap wood
9" x 14" scrap wood
Saber saw, scroll saw
Wood glue
Two 60" hinges
Wood screws
Screwdriver
Wood blocks (optional)
Acrylic paints: black, white, gray and orange
Paintbrushes
Sponge
Polyurethane finish

DRAW a 3" grid on a 60" x 48" sheet of smooth exterior ¼" plywood for witch, cat and crows to copy patterns. (If making graves, use a full sheet to have extra plywood.) Copy patterns, below, square by square, directly on the plywood. For graves, draw one about 17" x 23" with ghost, as shown, and another about 9" x 14" on scrap wood.

ROUGH-CUT plywood to separate pieces with a saber saw, then use fine blade on saw or scroll saw for details. Sand edges.

CUT stakes, if necessary, from scrap wood; glue and tack to bottom. Make a wood brace with pointed end to support witch. Attach to back with hinges (add wood blocks for screw length if necessary).

PAINT witch, cat and crows with black acrylic paint. Let dry. Then paint orange beaks and white eye on crows. Paint gravestones gray. Smudge with black and sponge on darker gray. Paint lines for cracks or outlines of ghost. Print message in black. Coat acrylic paint with a polyurethane finish.

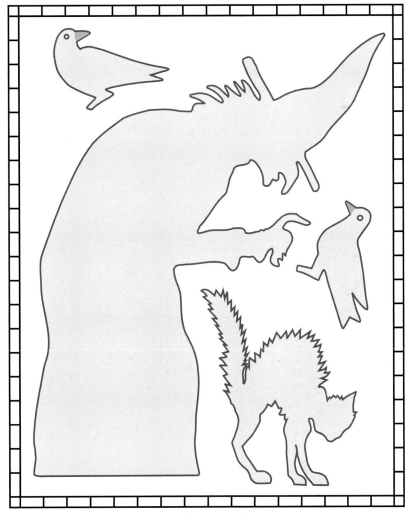

Each square = 3"

GRAVEYARD GHOSTS

Brown paper
Tacky glue (we used Aleene's Original)
Fiberfill stuffing or shredded paper
Lightweight cardboard
Acrylic paints: black, white and gray
Sand
Paintbrushes
Sheet of watercolor paper
Spanish moss

TRACE patterns, left. Cut 2 each of small (S), medium (M) and large (L) tombstones from brown paper.

GLUE pieces together in pairs with scant ¼"-wide line of glue at edge, leaving opening for stuffing and opening at each dot for wire. Let dry. (Note: Can be speed-dried on low setting at short intervals in microwave; watch to prevent scorching.)

STUFF lightly with fiberfill or shredded paper. Glue opening closed.

CUT 4" x 5" piece of cardboard as brace for each one. Fold in ¼" along inner edge; glue to back.

MIX a little sand into gray acrylic paint. Paint gravestones. When dry, lightly dab on black and white acrylic paint with sponge or brush. With fine brush, add dark gray lines for cracks with small brush. Paint message in black.

CUT ghosts' heads and hands from single sheet of watercolor or other heavy paper. Vary hands. Paint both sides white. Add gray streaks and black faces. Glue heads to back and hands to front of tombstones, folding edge of hands to back.

GLUE dried Spanish moss to bottom front of tombstones.

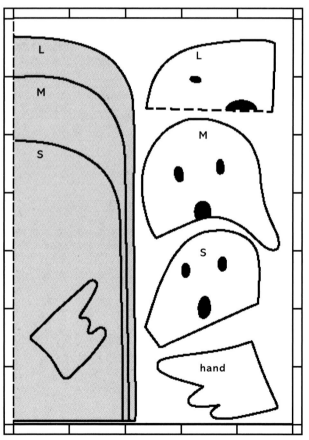

Each square = 1"

PUPPET PARADE 🅴

Cotton garden glove
Wax paper
Acrylic paints in assorted colors
Paintbrush
Fabric glue
Pompons, chenille stems, 7 mm movable eyes,
*   yarn, scraps of felt, ribbons*

STUFF the fingers of the glove with wax paper.

PAINT the fingers with acrylic paints. Let dry.

REMOVE wax paper. Using pinking shears or scissors, carefully cut off the glove's fingers at the knuckle.

GLUE on pompoms, chenille stems, movable eyes, yarn, felt and ribbon to create characters.

FINGER PUPPETS 🅴

Scraps of felt and patterned fabrics in
*   Halloween colors*
Fabric glue
*   Black dimensional fabric paint*
*   Yarn*
*   Several ¼" pompoms*
*   ½ yd of baby rickrack*
*   Small, sharp scissors*

TRACE pattern, left. Cut 2 from folded fabric, with broken line on fold, for each of 5 puppets. With right sides together, ¼" seam, stitch or glue sides, then hem. Turn right side out; press.

CUT 1½"-diam felt circle (or 2 glued together) for each head. Paint face, or cut and glue felt features. Add yarn hair to scarecrow and witch, pompom nose and rickrack whiskers to cat. Draw and cut felt hats for witch, scarecrow and ghost, and stem for pumpkin; glue.

COLORFUL CORN Ⓔ

Dress up your home with these cheery corn husks.

> *Posterboard*
> *Tissue papers: red, orange, yellow, purple and white*
> *Tacky glue (we used Aleene's Original)*
> *Natural paper-twist ribbon*
> *Raffia*

CUT corn cob shape from posterboard.

CUT sheets of red, orange, yellow, purple and white tissue paper into 4" squares and bunch to form "kernels."

GLUE to one side of the corn cutout, filling it completely. Cut three 18" lengths of paper twist. Untwist and trim to form husks.

LAY pieces so they overlap and insert "ear of corn" inside. Fold over edges at the bottom, twist and tie with raffia strip.

LITTLE GOBBLER ⓔ

Put these turkeys all around the house to get into a Thanksgiving frame of mind.

> *Construction paper in assorted colors*
> *Colored paper cup*
> *White glue*
> *Small wooden spoon*
> *Scrap of yellow or orange felt*
> *Yarn*
> *Black fine-point permanent marker*

CUT out 6" x 1" strips of colored paper, cutting a point at one end of each.

FORM a fan-like shape and glue or tape to back of colored cup.

CUT wing shapes from construction paper.

GLUE small wooden spoon to cup for the head.

GLUE on wings, felt beak and yarn mouth.

DRAW details with marker.

TURKEY-TROT ⓔ GARLAND

> *Tracing paper*
> *Deep-yellow or gold construction paper with coarse finish*
> *Craft knife*
> *Crayons: brown and rust*
> *Clear tape*

TRACE turkey shape, printed over text, onto tracing paper.

CUT construction paper into 5¼"-high strips.

FOLD each into an accordion shape 3¼" x 5¼".

TRANSFER turkey drawing to construction paper using a pencil. Make sure bottom feather is on fold so turkey shapes will be attached (see photo).

CUT out shape carefully using scissors or craft knife through all layers of folded paper.

DRAW feather and face details with crayons.

REPEAT to lengthen garland, attaching other garlands with tape.

NAPKIN HOLDERS

FOR EACH ONE

Brown and orange cardboard or heavy-weight construction paper
Hole punch
Scissors or craft knife
Tacky glue
Yellow paper
Brown fine-point permanent marker
Scrap of red felt or fabric
Chenille stem
Paper napkin in Thanksgiving colors

CUT out 3½"- to 4"-diam circle with diagonal base (see photo) from orange cardboard for turkey body.

PUNCH two holes 1¼" up from base and 1" apart on center for chenille stem.

CUT out turkey face shape (using photo as guide) from brown paper. It must cover the two holes.

PUNCH out two more holes from yellow paper and glue on for eyes; use marker for pupils.

CUT out two small yellow paper triangles and fold to make beak. Glue in place.

GLUE on scrap of felt or fabric for wattle.

FOLD napkin in half and then fold accordion-style.

INSERT both ends of chenille stem through holes and twist around napkin in back to hold, making sure turkey stands. Cut off excess with scissors.

GLUE turkey face to front, covering chenille stem.

TURKEY CENTERPIECE E

This gobbler is guaranteed to be the center of attention on a holiday table.

Construction paper in assorted colors
Paper bag
White glue
Red chenille stem

TRACE your hand on several colors of construction paper and cut out for feather shapes.

ROLL back top edge of paper bag and glue on feathers.

CUT out wings, head and pilgrim hat from construction paper. Attach to bag. Use a red chenille stem for the turkey's wattle.

THANKSGIVING PLACECARD Ⓔ

FOR EACH ONE

Two 7 mm movable eyes
Low-temp glue gun or tacky glue
Almond (in shell)
Small apple
1 Life Savers candy
Peanut (in shell)
Paper napkin
Small paper clip
Colored paper

GLUE movable eyes to almond and let dry. Glue Life Savers to front of apple and let dry. Glue almond to Life Savers and let dry. Glue peanut below almond for turkey's wattle.

UNFOLD napkin halfway, then fold back and forth accordion-style.

PUT a paper clip in the center of the folded napkin.

PULL ends of folded napkin together to make a fan; secure with a paper clip at top (see photo). Sit napkin behind turkey.

UNBEND one end of a paper clip and insert into apple. Use it to hold placecard. Cut placecard from colored paper.

PILGRIM'S PROGRESS Ⓔ

Oak tag
8"-wide terra-cotta pot
Scissors or craft knife
Mini glue gun
Terra-cotta spray (we used American Accents)
28" x 2" brown velvet ribbon or fabric
Metallic gold paper

CUT approximately 15"-diam circle from oak tag using a compass or bowl for guide.

TURN terra-cotta pot upside down, center on oak tag circle and trace.

CUT out inner circle ½" smaller in diameter than pot opening.

MAKE small slits about every ½" around the inner circle.

CUT a line between inner and outer circles. Overlap and glue back together to form beveled hat brim.

FOLD down inner circle slits and glue to inside of pot.

PAINT pot and brim with terra-cotta spray. Let dry.

GLUE ribbon or fabric band around pot.

CUT buckle shape from gold paper backed with oak tag and glue to hat band.

SNOWMAN CARD Ⓔ

Blue watercolor or acrylic and orange acrylic paints
Small paintbrushes
2" x 3" white felt sheet and scrap of black felt
Watercolor or art paper
Sparkles Glitter Writer (we used GW 212 by Duncan)
Blank 5" x 7" card
White glue
Toothpick
Black fine-point permanent marker

TRACE snowman and hat half-patterns, left. Cut from felt.

PAINT watercolor paper blue. Let dry. Brush on glitter. Cut 2¾" x 3½" rectangle from the painted paper; center and glue to card front; weight to dry flat.

CUT ⅝" toothpick tip for snowman's nose; paint orange. Dot on eyes and mouth with marker.

GLUE snowman and hat to background. Cut and glue on a plaid scarf. Draw stick arms with marker. Glue nose on flat.

MAGNETIC ANGEL CARD

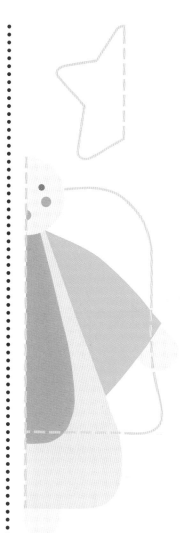

White posterboard: 7½" x 10½" for card,
   2" square for star
Craft knife and straightedge
8" x 11" red pin-dot background fabric
Large needle, small needle
⅛"-wide satin ribbon: 1½ yds green and 8" red
Tracing paper
Transfer paper
Scraps of muslin and assorted fabrics for angel
Acrylic paints: black, rose and golden-yellow
Small paintbrushes
Paper-backed fusible web
Black fine-point permanent marker
4½" x 5½" white felt
Tacky glue
10" gold metallic wired stem
12" string or embroidery floss for hair
2" x 1½" flat magnet

SCORE center 5½" line of posterboard and fold away from cut for card. Fuse background fabric to outside, following manufacturer's directions and maintaining card fold. With craft knife and straightedge, trim even with card.

DRAW a line ½" from edges inside front; with large needle poke a hole every ¼" for sewing. Starting in upper left corner with smaller needle, sew ribbon running stitch in holes; tie bow.

TRACE angel and star half-patterns, right. Outline angel on felt; do not cut. Fuse web to back of fabrics for angel details. Trace separate patterns whole on paper backing, adding underlap to hand, feet and sleeves. Cut from fabric. Paint face on muslin head with small brush or toothpick.

FUSE posterboard squares together for star; cut star; paint yellow. When dry, write message on star with marker.

FUSE wings to felt angel, then other pieces all together. Cut out angel. Glue magnet to back.

BEND glitter stem to form arc. Glue angel's hands ½" from ends and bend ends back at right angle. Wind string or floss around finger for hair; remove and tie around center. Glue to head. Glue bow to neck.

POSITION angel on card; poke a hole behind each hand; insert and bend stem to hold angel on card.

FELT WARDROBE ORNAMENTS ⓘ

*Felt: 3 red and 1 white 9" x 12" scraps in gold
   and black*
Needle and black embroidery floss
3 strands dental floss
1 yd 20-gauge wire
Wire snips
White glue
1" x 2½" red gingham
3 tiny black buttons

ENLARGE patterns labeled "F," opposite (see *How to Enlarge Patterns,* page 144). Cut from felt.

STITCH tiny straight stitches with 3 strands floss on white trims and cuffs.

HANGERS (MAKE 4): Cut 9" wire. Center wire along bottom of hanger pattern and bend into shape; trim excess.

JACKET: Glue cuffs and front trims to one jacket piece, brushing glue on smoothly and weighting pieces to dry. Glue trims, cuffs and collar to back piece. Glue front to back, with hanger between them at neckline.

PANTS: For each of 3 pairs, glue cuffs even with lower edge to 1 piece for back and the other for front. With buckle: Glue belt, buckle and inner buckle to front, even with upper edge. Glue pants together with hanger sandwiched between. With drop drawer: Cut 3-sided drop drawer in 1 pants piece, following pattern. Glue gingham behind drawer to wrong side of other piece. Glue pants together over hanger. Sew a button to hold up right-hand top corner of drop drawer; fold left corner down and stitch. With suspenders: Glue or tack 1 end of suspenders to pants front ¼" in from sides and ⅜" below top with button. Glue pants together. Cross suspenders, attach ends to back and slip over hanger. Hang clothes individually or from a twine clothesline as a garland.

PAPER GIFT TAGS ●

Construction papers: red, white, black, yellow and green (we used Canson)
Craft knife
White craft glue

ENLARGE patterns labeled "P", right (see *How to Enlarge Patterns,* page 144). Cut from colored paper with knife guided along straightedge or with scissors.

JACKET: Glue cuffs and trims to fronts. Glue sleeves and ¼" along sides of fronts to back. Fold fronts out to side, write message inside; reclose.

PANTS: Cut out pants with left edge on fold. Glue cuffs and belt with buckle to front. Write message inside.

SOCKS: Cut out socks on fold; glue heel and toe patches to front.

HAT: Glue on cuff. Fold down top and glue on star.

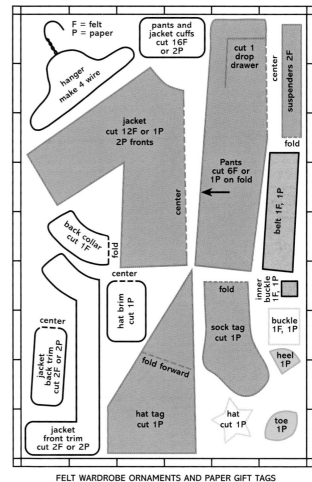

FELT WARDROBE ORNAMENTS AND PAPER GIFT TAGS
Each square = 1"

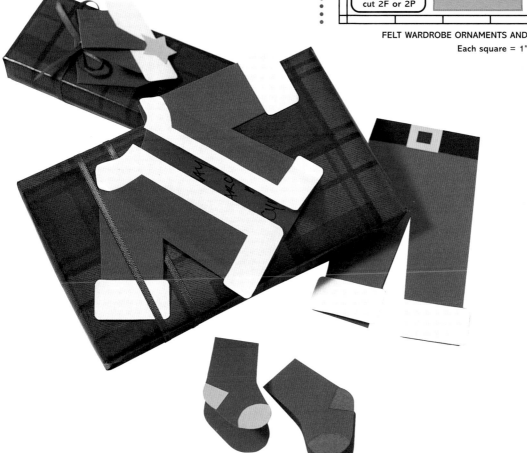

PLAYFUL SANTAS

FOR 12

6 jumbo craft sticks or tongue depressors
Craft knife
Acrylic paints: red, white, flesh and black
Small round and flat paintbrushes
Drill with ³⁄₁₆" bit
Tracing paper
Toothpick
Tacky glue (we used Aleene's Original)
1 each 9" x 12" red, white and black felt sheets
12 red 10" wired chenille stems

CUT 2½" from each end of craft sticks with craft knife for 12 Santa bodies.

PAINT pieces red on both sides.

TRACE Santa, mitten and boot patterns, right. Stack and tape painted pieces; drill ³⁄₁₆" holes for legs at lower dots.

SCRIBBLE on back of pattern with soft pencil, then trace on front of body. Paint face flesh color. Mix with red to add rosy nose and cheeks. Dot black eyes with toothpick. Paint white beard, fur, brows and mustache; black belt.

CUT 1 each 4" chenille for arms, 6" for legs. Cut long ½"-wide strips of red felt. Glue 1 end, then wind strip tightly along chenille to cover it; glue end. Insert leg from front in 1 hole halfway and out the other. Glue center of arms to back.

CUT 2 black boots and white mittens. Fold over ends of arms and legs; glue.

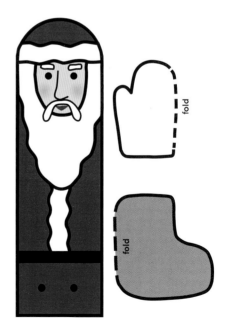

POPCORN BAG Ⓔ

Prepare cutouts, but pop popcorn and assemble bags at the last minute.

> *Tracing paper*
> *Construction paper: red, white and black*
> *Tacky glue*
> *Popcorn*
> *Ziptop plastic sandwich bag*
> *Low-temp glue gun*

ENLARGE patterns, below (see *How to Enlarge Patterns*, page 144). Trace full-size patterns and cut from construction paper. Also cut 2 white eyebrows. Glue pompom and brim to hat.

POP corn. Let cool.

FILL bag with fresh popcorn. Seal firmly.

APPLY glue to back of cutouts, then attach pieces to bag.

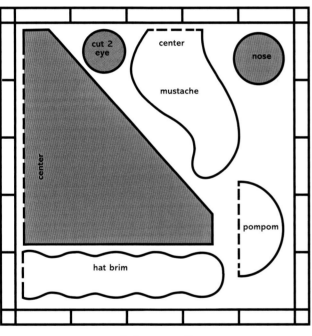

cut 2 eye

center

nose

mustache

center

pompom

hat brim

Each square = 1"

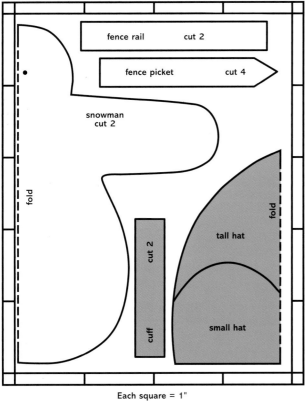

SNOWMAN ORNAMENTS

FOR EACH ONE

Two 6¼" x 5" pieces of white fabric or lightweight canvas
Scraps of colored fleece
Fiberfill stuffing
Acrylic paints: orange, black and assorted colors
Toothpick or bamboo skewer for nose
Fabric glue
¼" pompom
Cinnamon sticks
Liquitex Liquigems Opal or glue and glitter
Low-temp glue gun
Tiny accessories
Embroidery thread

FENCE

3 craft or ice cream sticks
Garden shears
Low-temp glue gun
White acrylic paint
Twigs
Spanish moss
Duncan Snow Accents

TRACE patterns, left. Cut fabric snowman and fleece hat, cuffs and scarf.

STITCH snowman with ⅛" seam allowance, right sides together, leaving bottom open. Clip curves. Turn right side out. Stuff; sew closed.

PAINT ¾" skewer or toothpick tip orange for nose. Let dry. Cut tip off. With other end, paint black dot eyes and mouth. Let dry. Glue nose on.

PAINT ¾" color at end of arms for mittens.

STITCH hat side closed, wrong side out. Turn. Fold brim up.

GLUE hat to head, pompom to hat, cuffs around mittens, cinnamon stick(s) to bottom, accessory to hand.

STITCH embroidery thread through back of head for hanger.

BRUSH thin coat of Opal (or glue and glitter) at random lightly over everything. Let dry. Tie ¾" x 11" scarf around neck.

FENCE: Cut four 2½" pickets and two 3" rails from craft sticks. Glue pickets to rails. Paint white. Glue cinnamon and twigs to base, snowman and fence to base, moss around fence. Add snow; dry. Add glitter.

---

fence rail cut 2

fence picket cut 4

snowman
cut 2

fold

fold

cut 2

tall hat

cuff

small hat

Each square = 1"

WOOD-BLOCK ELF ORNAMENT (A)

2" wooden cube
Acrylic paints (we used FolkArt Ivory White,
  Shamrock and Crimson)
Small pointed brush or Q-tip for dots
Grosgrain ribbon: 11" each 3/8"-wide green
  and blue, 27" of 1/4"-wide red
Low-temp glue gun
1 1/2" wooden bead
1 1/2" nail
4" x 5" fabric for hat
1/4" tan and 1/2" red pompoms
Flat paintbrush
Black fine-point permanent marker or paint
10" blue embroidery floss

PAINT cube white. Let dry. Paint on green dots.

WRAP 9" red ribbon around cube one way; wrap another around empty sides; glue ends at top.

GLUE center of blue ribbon to top for arms. Cut green ribbon in half; glue to bottom for legs. Trim ends diagonally.

GLUE and nail bead to center top.

PRESS under 1/4" on 4" ends of fabric for hat. Wrap to fit head; glue sides closed. Gather one end and glue on pompom. Glue to head.

DRAW black eyes and mouth; paint pink cheeks (red and white). Glue on tan pompom nose.

GLUE red bow under chin. Fold hat to side. At center top, stitch 3"-long floss loop for hanging.

FELT GINGERBREAD MAN ORNAMENT (B)

9" x 12" brown felt sheet
Tracing paper
Air-soluble fabric marker
Dressmaker's white carbon paper or other
  transfer paper
Shiny White Plaid Fashion Fabric Paint
½ yd each of ⅜" red polka-dot grosgrain and
  ⅛" green satin ribbons
Embroidery needle
Red or green embroidery floss
Fiberfill stuffing
Pinking shears

CUT felt in half into 6" x 9" blocks.

TRACE gingerman half-pattern, right. Transfer outline (seamline) with marker to center of one block; transfer major clothing lines with carbon.

PAINT designs (not seamline), starting at top, after first practising to use. Let dry.

PIN blocks together right side out. Thread needle with floss; knot end. Hiding knot between layers, sew running stitches along seamline; stuff from side before completing round.

TRIM edges with pinking shears.

GLUE or tack ends of 2" red ribbon to top back for loop. Tie bow of red and green ribbons held together; tack or glue to top front.

BUTTONED-UP TREE (C)

Tracing and dressmaker's carbon papers
Two 4½" x 6" pieces green calico
Green thread and embroidery floss
Pinking shears
Fiberfill stuffing
½ yd of ⅛"-wide red ribbon
15 buttons in assorted colors and sizes

TRACE tree half-pattern, right. Transfer with carbon to front of one piece of fabric. Pin pieces together right side out.

STITCH around tree on line, stuffing before end. Trim edge with pinking shears.

SEW on buttons with floss. Tack 2" ribbon loop at top and bow to trunk.

TENNIS-BALL ELF ORNAMENT (D)

Tennis ball
Craft knife
10" circle of Christmas-print fabric
1½" wooden bead
Tacky glue or low-temp glue gun
Acrylic paints (we used FolkArt Ivory White,
  Crimson and Black)
4" x 5" fabric for hat
Small round paintbrush
¾" red pompom
11" each of ⅜"-wide blue and green
  grosgrain ribbons
10" of ¾"-wide checked ribbon
Thread
Embroidery floss for loop

SLIT ¾" "X" into top of ball. Wrap with fabric and push edges into opening. Glue bead over opening.

PRESS under ¼" on 4" ends of fabric for hat. Gather one end with running stitches. Wrap to fit head; glue sides closed. Glue to head.

PAINT eyes and cheeks. Glue on red pompom nose. Gather one edge of checked ribbon and glue around neck for collar.

CUT grosgrain ribbons in half; glue on for arms and legs. Sew 3"-long floss loop for hanging at top.

PATCHWORK HOLLY BALL ORNAMENT (E)

Fourteen 1½" x 13" strips of assorted fabrics
Thread
Tennis ball
Craft knife
Tracing paper
Green felt remnant
Three ½" red pompoms
Embroidery floss for loop

STITCH fabrics, with right sides together, ⅛" seam allowance, side by side to form stripes.

CUT 1½"-wide lengths across stripes to have rows of squares. Stitch together, alternating colors, for patchwork.

SLIT ¾" "X" in top of tennis ball. Wrap fabric around ball, fold flat as needed and push edges into slits.

TRACE pattern printed over text and cut 3 holly leaves from green felt. Glue leaves, then pompom "berries" to top. Sew 3"-long floss loop for hanging at top.

PINECONE SKIER ORNAMENT (F)

FOR EACH ONE

3"- to 4"-long pinecone
Acrylic paints: yellow, orange, white and black
2 toothpicks
Felt: 2" x 3½" for hat and ¾" x 6" for scarf
Low-temp glue gun
1"-diam wooden bead
6" blue or green chenille stem
Black fine-point permanent marker or paint for face
Two ⅜" x 4" strips of stiff colored paper

PAINT tips of cone scales for body and toothpicks for ski poles. Let dry.

ROLL cone-shaped felt hat; glue sides closed; trim lower edge even. Glue to bead.

DRAW or paint dot eyes and nose and curved mouth on bead.

GLUE center of chenille stem under scales at top of cone for arms.

GLUE scarf around top, crossed in front (slit back to help curve). Glue head to top. Glue ends of arms around ski poles.

CUT rounded point at one end of each paper strip for skis. Glue to bottom. Sew 3"-long floss loop for hanging at top.

CLOTH-AND-PAPER QUILTS ORNAMENT (G)

Graph paper
Scraps of tiny calico-print, dotted and checked fabrics
Rotary cutter, mat and ruler
½ yd of Pellon Wonder-Under Transfer Web
5" square of stiff red or white paper
Spray adhesive or white glue
½ yd of red or green ⅜" satin ribbon
Low-temp glue gun
Fiskars scallop and lace paper-edger scissors

CUT a 3½" square from graph paper. Use as a pattern to cut a square from lightest-color fabric with rotary cutter (see 9-Patch and Log-Cabin diagrams, below).

IRON web to back of fabrics, following manufacturer's instructions; leave paper on. Draw patterns and cut fabric strips and squares to fit, letting background print be part of design. Peel off backing, arrange pieces on background; iron in place.

GLUE fabric block to paper. Trim paper, about ¼" from fabric, with paper edger.

GLUE ends of 4" ribbon to back at corner for loop. Glue 3" bow in front of loop.

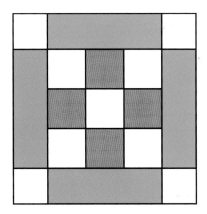

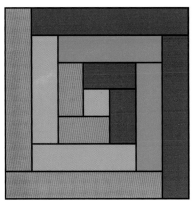

MEMORY TREE

20" x 30" plywood or other support
Sturdy sawtooth or other hanger (optional)
Medium and fine sandpaper
White acrylic paint (we used FolkArt Wicker White)
Clean rag
½"- to 1"-wide masking tape
Souvenirs, photos, tickets, toys, alphabet stickers, etc.
Assorted buttons, flat-backed acrylic beads and gems as ornaments
1 yd each green and red ¼" faceted plastic beads
Strong tacky glue (we used Magna-Tac)
Toy deputy-sheriff badge for star (optional)

INSTALL hanger on back of wood centered 6" below 20" side (this will be top of frame). Sand wood edges; dust off residue. Rub paint onto front and edges with rag. Let dry.

OUTLINE a simple pine tree shape on front of board lightly with masking tape. Arrange, then glue souvenir objects and gems inside tree and trunk.

REMOVE tape and replace outline with glued-on strings of beads, starting at top on each side. Fill any gaps with gems. Glue a large bead or button to tip of each branch and star badge to top if you wish.

CANDY CANES

Tracing paper
Transfer paper
Card stock for template
Black fine-point permanent marker
Fun Foam sheets
Buttons or flat gems
Strong tacky glue (we used Magna-Tac)
or low-temp glue gun

TRACE cane pattern, left. Tape to card stock and cut through both layers to have a template for making multiples.

OUTLINE cane on foam with marker; cut from foam. Glue buttons to front. When glue sets, repeat on back.

PAPER ANGEL ❶

2½" wood ball for head
Flesh-colored acrylic paint (we used FolkArt
  Rose White)
Tacky glue or low-temp glue gun
Black fine-point permanent marker
Pink blush
8" x 15" oak tag cardboard
Stapler or adhesive tape
Three 9" x 30" sheets varied rice papers for clothes
Spray adhesive
Gold paper trim
2 white chenille stems
6" of 1¼" gold mesh ribbons
12" of ⅛" gold wire-edge
10" x 12" gold paper
Scrap of white tulle
Yarn for hair
Scrap white card

ENLARGE wing and dove patterns, right (see *How to Enlarge Patterns,* page 144).

PAINT ball. Let dry. Wind yarn in 1 layer around a 3"-wide cardboard strip. Sew together on 1 side. Remove; cut other side. Glue across head. Add bangs. Draw face with marker. Blush cheeks.

CUT 15" x 8" semicircle from oak tag. Hold at center of straight edge and overlap sides to form cone with slightly open top and base about 5½" diam. Staple or tape side closed. Trim edge if necessary.

CUT same shape 9" long from rice paper. Spray-glue to cone, turning lower edge inside.

GATHER long edge of one paper for dress by pleating or folding; glue to top of cone. Gather another paper for cloak; glue at top with open front. Trim front with gold paper trim.

FOLD chenille stems in half. Roll same paper as for cloak over them to make sleeves; glue side closed. Cut and glue oak-tag hands to folded chenille ends. Glue arms to top back; bend forward.

WIND thread or wire around center of two 3" strips of mesh ribbon. Glue to neck. Top with tulle bow.

CUT 2 gold wings (double layer if necessary). Pleat straight end; glue to back. Form halo from wire ribbon, leaving 2" end. Glue end to back of head.

CUT dove from card stock. Insert wings through slit in body. Glue dove to hand.

GINGERMAN DOLL 🅘

Felt: ½ yd tan, 9" x 12" white, ⅛ yd green
Thread
Fiberfill stuffing
¾ yd of *white baby rickrack*
Fabric glue
1 red ¾" pompom
Ribbon: ¼ yd of 2½" green check and ½ yd
    of ⅜" red satin
Buttons: 2 black ¼" half-balls (eyes), 3 red ⅝"

NOTE: *Use fabric paint instead of buttons to make doll for a child under three years old.*

ENLARGE doll and cane patterns, left (see *How to Enlarge Patterns*, page 144). Adding ¼" seam allowance all around, cut 2 each from tan felt.

STITCH pieces in pairs with right sides together, leaving an opening for turning. Clip curves; turn right side out. Stuff firmly. Hand-sew opening closed.

CUT white felt mouth and four 5" rickrack strips. Glue to doll as in photo. Sew on pompom nose, eyes and buttons. Fold ends of 8" checked ribbon to center back for bow tie; wrap short strip around center; glue or sew under chin.

CUT 2" x 6" green felt for hat. Roll tightly lengthwise for solid crown; glue. Trace top; cut circle and glue on. Cut two 3"-diam circles for brim. Glue together. Glue crown to center; glue hat to head.

WIND red ribbon on cane; glue ends.

CARD HOLDER 🅔

42 spring-clip clothespins
2 green acrylic paints (we used FolkArt Shamrock [S]
    and Evergreen [E])
Small flat paintbrush
Wire hanger or sturdy wire, wire cutter, pliers
    (needlenose helpful)
14 red and 28 green 9 x 6 mm pony beads
Tie wire
1 yd of 2¾" red ribbon

PAINT 21 clothespins each with S and E.

CUT hook off hanger. Form open circle and a small ½" loop at one end to hang wreath, using pliers.

STRING red bead, S pin, green bead, E pin, green bead, S pin, red bead, E pin; continue alternating pin colors with 2 green beads and 1 red throughout.

HOOK ends together or tie with thin wire. Tie bow. Wire bow over joining.

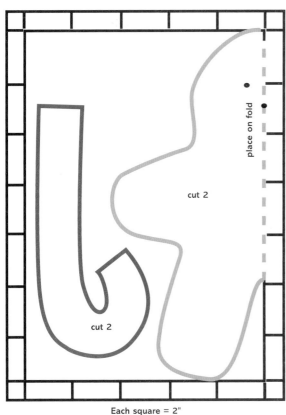

place on fold

cut 2

cut 2

Each square = 2"

KEEPSAKE BOX

Hexagonal papier-mâché dome box
Spray gesso (we used Krylon)
Acrylic paint (we used FolkArt Lipstick Red)
White paint pen
Scraps of 2 to 7 different papers
Holiday or other miniatures for dome
Spray adhesive or Mod Podge
Tacky glue or low-temp glue gun

REMOVE lid of dome box and apply gesso. Let dry. Paint lid red. Pencil "Do not open until Christmas" or another phrase around lid side. Paint letters white with white pen.

CUT paper to cover each side of box, adding 1" to width of 3 strips and to length of all.

GLUE the 3 wider strips to alternate sides of box with spray, trimming corners and gluing ½" ends inside box and under bottom. Glue the flush strips to remaining sides.

COVER base of dome with paper. Glue miniatures to base arranged to fit under dome. Glue arrangement inside lid.

SANTA-IN-THE-BOX ①

SIZE: *33" tall*

> *18" square corrugated cardboard*
> *Cardboard box (18" square x 16" high)*
> *Low-temp glue gun*
> *Two 30" x 40" sheets corrugated cardboard*
>   *or single sheet ¼" plywood*
> *Packing tape*
> *Transfer paper*
> *Craft knife*
> *Saber saw*
> *30" x 40" each white fabric and quilt batting*
> *Acrylic paints (we used FolkArt Lipstick Red,*
>   *School Bus Yellow, Black, Sky Blue, Green,*
>   *Dark Brown)*
> *Flat and round paintbrushes*
> *2 yds of 1¼" and 1 yd of 2¾" red ribbon*

GLUE cardboard square to inside of one of the upper box flaps. Push other flaps into box. Tape bottom closed. If using cardboard sheets for Santa, glue into 2 layers with dots of glue throughout. Draw 4" grid on cardboard or plywood.

ENLARGE Santa pattern, right (see *How to Enlarge Patterns,* page 144). Cut cardboard with craft knife; saw wood with saber saw. Cut shape from batting. Cut 3" larger all around from fabric.

GLUE batting lightly to front of Santa. Stretch fabric over batting and glue excess to back, clipping slits into edges so fabric lies flat. Transfer inner shapes.

PAINT Santa, leaving white fabric for white areas. Paint box brown inside and out. When dry, with lid open, glue ribbon taut from inside box near front to lid sides, to hold lid up. Paint green squares and yellow "Merry Christmas" on box as shown.

CUT 9" x 18" doubled cardboard or plywood. Glue or screw upper 9" to lower back of Santa to add height. Glue a 9" x 12" 85-degree triangle on edge to back for stand. Support with scrap as needed.

Each square = 4"

PENGUIN FAMILY Ⓔ

FOR EACH ONE

3½" x 11" balsa wood
Transfer paper
Craft knife
Yellow, orange, gray and black permanent felt-tip
*   markers (2 tip sizes useful)*
Paint for stake (optional)
Craft stick or floral marker for stake
Low-temp glue gun or strong tacky glue
*   (we used Magna-Tac)*

ENLARGE patterns, left (see *How to Enlarge Patterns,* page 144). Transfer to wood and cut with craft knife. Cut separate wings, baby, mother's head and feet.

COLOR with markers, following pattern outlines for shapes and photo for colors. Leave tan areas (chests) unpainted. Start with a light-colored area; outline shape with small-tip pen, then fill with wide-tip pen. Let dry before adding adjacent color. Color black sections last. Paint stake.

GLUE wings and other parts in position. Glue stake to back and insert in plant, or brace penguin with scraps of wood to stand alone.

Each square = 2"

CHENILLE STEM Ⓔ
WREATH

15"–17" grapevine wreath
Matte black spray paint
Black glitter
Beacon Fabri-tac Adhesive
Chenille stems: orange, lime green, silver, white
*   and purple*
Small pompoms in various colors
2 yds each ½"-wide black and orange ribbon

SPRAY wreath with black paint in a well-ventilated and covered area. Immediately sprinkle black glitter onto wet paint; let dry.

BEND chenille stems into shapes. Glue stems and pompoms to wreath.

TIE ribbon bow to wreath.

BUNNY GARLAND

Construction paper or card stock
Black medium-point permanent marker
Acrylic paints in assorted colors
Eleven white ½" pompoms
Tacky glue (we used Aleene's Original)

TRACE blue bunny pattern, below, onto left end of a 4" x 26" strip of paper, or trace 11 in a row, attached at eggs and feet, onto card stock.

FOLD paper accordion-style to width of bunny, or cut shapes attached on card stock, then fold.

PRINT 1 letter of "Happy Easter" on front of each bunny with marker.

COLOR eggs with acrylic paint or markers.

GLUE ¼" pompom tails below letters.

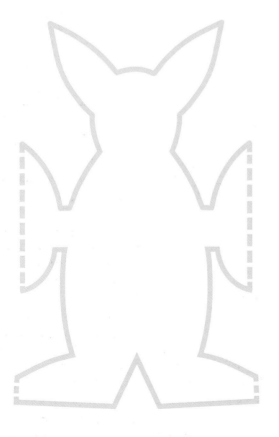

BUNNY TOTE

Two 6" x 9" pastel felt sheets
White felt
Yarn or fabric glue
24" of ¼"-wide satin ribbon
Safety pin
¾" white or pastel pompom
Tacky glue

CUT 2 pieces 6" x 9" pastel felt (or desired size) for bag front and back. Trace pink bunny half-pattern, below. Cut 1 from white felt.

STITCH or glue bunny to bag front, centered ¾" above lower edge. With right sides out, topstitch front to back along side and lower edges.

CUT ⅜"-high vertical slits for ribbon, starting ½" from side edge. Cut through both layers at once, placing slits about 1¼" below top and every 1¼" across bag (10 slits). Starting at side and using a safety pin as a guide, weave satin ribbon through slits. Gather top and tie bow.

ATTACH a ¾" white or pastel pompom tail with tacky glue.

STACKED BUNNY

*3 round chipwood or other boxes in graduated sizes
  (ours are 4¹⁄₂"-, 5"- and 5³⁄₄"-diam)*
Acrylic paints: white, black, pink and blue
FolkArt Crackle Medium
#2 round, ¹⁄₄" stencil and ¹⁄₂" flat brushes
Scraps of blue and yellow paper ribbon and canvas
Artificial flower
6"-diam straw hat
Yellow and pink ¹⁄₂" buttons
Low-temp glue gun
Tacky glue

BOXES: Mix a pale gray from drops of black paint in white. Thin slightly with water and brush 1 coat on each box. Let dry. Apply crackle medium on boxes and lids separately, following manufacturer's instructions. Let dry. Paint a thin coat pure white to crackle lightly.

BUNNY: On one side, following photo, lightly pencil eye dots (on lid), nose and mouth on upper box, paws on middle box and legs on lowest box. Paint lines black. Let dry. With stencil brush, dab on pink cheeks and lines to define toes. Paint blue whiskers and white eye highlights.

EARS: Cut two 4"-long rabbit ears from canvas. Paint pink on fronts. Pleat at center bottom; glue to sides of hat crown. Add flower. Glue hat to top; bow and buttons to front.

EASTER TREE

5" high x 6"-diam clay terra-cotta pot
Acrylic enamel paints (we used Apple Barrel Gloss
Dandelion Yellow, Lanier Blue and Raspberry for
pot, plus Spring and Seafoam greens and Deep
Purple for eggs)
Foam brush
Household sponge
Small brushes for eggs
1³⁄₈" wooden eggs
15" branch with smaller branches for tree (or a
15" x ³⁄₈" dowel or straight branch for trunk and
12 paper-wrapped 18" wires for branches)
24-gauge wire
Wire snips
Green spray paint (we used Krylon Teal Green)
Green plastic floral foam sheet or chunks
1½ yds of ⁷⁄₈"-wide pink and blue ribbon
10" of ¼"-wide ribbon for each egg
Basket grass or live grass in sod
Tacky glue

PAINT pot yellow with foam brush. When dry, sponge on 1¼" checkerboard squares, alternating rows of raspberry and blue. Paint eggs assorted-color stripes, half egg at a time; prop to dry (a good place is the dent between egg cups on a cardboard egg carton).

WRAP center of 6 paper-covered wires at intervals around dowel or straight branch, starting about 9" above bottom, if not using natural branch as tree. Bind joints with wire to keep these branches from slipping. Wrap short paper-covered wire branches around the others to fill out tree.

SPRAY-PAINT tree, following manufacturer's instructions. Let dry. Wedge foam into pot and tree into foam. Glue ribbon around pot rim. Tie separate bow; cut wedge in ends; glue to pot. To hang eggs, glue ends of 3¼" ribbon to top for loop; glue bow below loop.

COVER foam with basket grass or growing grass in soil. Decorate tree with eggs. Add pompom chicks and paper butterflies if desired (see instructions, right).

POMPOM CHICKS 🄴

FOR EACH ONE

1" to 1½" yellow pompom
¾" to 1" pompom (optional)
Tacky glue
Low-temp glue gun
1" orange wired chenille stem
Two 5 mm movable eyes

GLUE 1" to 1½" yellow pompom with tacky glue to make large chick. Glue ¾" to 1" pompom for smaller chick, or trim the larger one.

BEND the strip of orange chenille stem into V shape for foot. Cut ¼"-long snip of stem for beak. Glue feet under body, and beak and movable eyes to head.

PAPER BUTTERFLIES 🄴

FOR EACH ONE

6" square origami paper or other thin paper
White glue
4¾" of wired chenille stem
Low-temp glue gun

CUT a 6" square of origami paper in half. Fold 1 piece in half with short ends together; fold in half again in same direction to have 4 layers to make 1 butterfly.

TRACE butterfly wing shape, below. With broken line of pattern on last fold, cut around wings through all layers, leaving fold uncut. Open to have 2 layers. Glue layers together using white glue or stick glue.

BEND 1¼" length of wired chenille in half for antennae. Glue with ends extending at center top between the pointed wings. Fold 3½" chenille stem in half over center of butterfly between wings for body; glue in place.

CHICKS-IN-THE-SHELL ❶

FOR EACH ONE

Large or medium raw egg (off-white or brown if available)
White glue
Scraps of yellow sweatshirt or fleece fabric, orange felt and fiberfill stuffing
14" of ¼"-wide ribbon
6 yellow marabou feathers
Low-temp glue gun
1½" square of ¼" plywood or heavy cardboard for base
Acrylic paints: blue, pink, aqua, black and purple
½" flat and #4 round brushes
Two 5 mm movable eyes

CUT and break egg gently in half. Wash and dry. Coat inside with water-thinned white glue; let dry. Snap off shell edges if too uneven or if top half is too large.

TRACE chick half-pattern, printed over text. Adding ¼" seam allowance, cut 2 chicks from yellow fabric. With right sides together, stitch edges, leaving bottom open. Clip curves. Turn right side out. Stuff. Sew or glue closed. Tie bow around neck.

CUT felt beak. Fold diagonally; clip, press or glue to hold crease; glue to face as per pattern. From underside, poke small hole in center of top half of egg. Glue feather into hole and shell to head. Glue feathers into lower shell showing at edges; add chick. Hot-glue egg to base.

PAINT base purple. With tip of small brush, paint black line in center of mouth fold and colored dots on shell. Glue eyes on.

TABLE BUNNIES ❶

FOR EACH ONE

Two 3" or 4" straw hats
Acrylic paints (we used FolkArt Titanium White, Pure Black, French Blue and Pink)
½" flat and 000 round paintbrushes
6" wired chenille stem
Scraps of thick (70 lb) nylon fishing line, white and pink fabric, white Fun Foam sheet and stiff white cardboard
Low-temp glue gun
14" of ¼"-⅜" ribbon
Small flat button
Two 6 mm movable eyes
Tacky glue (we used Aleene's Original)
Thick needle
Fishing line

PAINT brim and crown of one hat 2 coats white, letting each coat dry. Paint ⅔ of brim blue, leaving ⅓ white for shoulders. Paint pink nose, black mouth on center top of crown.

CUT other hat in half; bend brim back. Set aside.

TRACE ear pattern, below. Cut 2 each from pink and white fabric, reversing 1 each. Stitch in pairs, wrong side out with ¼" seam, leaving bottoms open. Turn right side out. Cut chenille in half. Bend tips and insert to stiffen ears. With pink facing front, glue lower edges of ears to back edge of half-hat crown.

CUT 1½" x 5" white fabric on bias for hatband. Fold under ⅜" on long edges. Glue across half-hat crown (for placecard, print name on band first with a felt-tip marker).

GLUE half-hat to bunny's head, trimming as needed to fit. Glue ribbon across neckline, folding ends under. Tie bow; glue to front. Add button below.

CUT a tiny pair of buck teeth in one piece from Fun Foam; glue. Bend ears. Glue on eyes.

POKE 3 holes in each side of nose with needle. Insert 2" fishing line whiskers; hot-glue at back.

CUT 1¼" x 5" cardboard for stand; taper sides to ⅝" at top. Glue top to center top of back. Bend outward below glue and near base to stand.

CLIP ON RABBITS

Brighten up any Easter basket with this adorable clip-on rabbit.

> *Colored heavyweight scrapbook paper*
> *Fine-point permanent markers*
> *1" pompom*
> *Tacky Glue (we used Aleene's Original)*
> *¼ yd of ¼" checked ribbon*
> *Spring-clips clothespin*

DRAW rabbit shape on colored paper, using photo left as guide. Cut out. Draw eyes, nose and mouth on face.

GLUE pompom to back for tail. Tie ribbon into bow, glue at neck.

GLUE clothespin behind rabbit.

BUNNY BUDDIES

FOR EACH ONE

> *Colored construction paper*
> *2 cardboard tubes*
> *Double-stick adhesive tape*
> *Tacky glue (we used Aleene's Original)*
> *Dimensional paint*
> *Printed decorative paper*
> *Two 5 mm movable eyes*
> *1" pompom*

ROLL equal lengths of colored paper around two cardboard tubes and tape ends. Glue the tubes together (see photo, left).

CUT out two matching ears and glue on. Draw whiskers and mouth with dimensional paint. Glue on movable eyes and pompom tail. Cut small paper triangle for nose; glue in place.

CUT construction paper to length of tube, making it wide enough to fit around tube. Wrap and glue paper to tube. Cover both tubes in same way.

CUT printed paper to fit each tube end. Tape in place. Glue tubes together.

CUT ears from both papers; glue layers together, then glue between tubes.

PAINTED SIGN

5" x 14" piece of ¾" pine
Jigsaw
Acrylic paints (we used Plaid Folk Art Green,
*   Harvest Gold, Lavender, Primrose, Sunny Yellow*
*   and Winter White)*
Paintbrushes
Sponge
Egg, half-egg, lamb, chick in the shell and rabbit
*   wooden craft cutouts*
Wood glue
White thumbtacks
Natural color raffia

CUT pine board into a gentle arch with the jigsaw.

PAINT the board pink; sponge some primrose around the edges; paint "Happy Easter" in white. Paint each wood cutout with a checkerboard design using one light and one darker color (the backs can be a solid color).

GLUE tulips (we made using half cutouts of eggs) to the sides of the board.

CUT four 10" lengths of raffia; string through holes in wood cutouts. Space 4 thumbtacks along the bottom edge of the board, push halfway in, tie on raffia with a bow then push the tacks securely into the board. Cut a 16" length of raffia for the hanger and secure with tacks behind tulips.

BUNNY FACES

Bristol boards: blue, pink and white
Small paper plates: pink, blue and white
Scissors and patterned scissors
Construction paper
Tacky glue (we used Aleene's Original)
Black fine-point permanent marker

CUT ears, about 6" high from bristol board, using color to match paper plate. Cut inner ears from contrasting bristol board. Layer and glue ears together, then glue ears behind upper fold on plate.

CUT pink cheeks in contrasting colors using decorative scissors. Cut noses in contrasting colors. Glue all pieces to face.

DRAW mouth and eyes using marker.

YARD BUNNIES

FOR EACH ONE

½ sheet of ½"- or ¾"-thick wood
Saber saw
Wood glue
Brads
Hammer
Acrylic paints (we used Delta Ceramcoat White, Pink Parfait, Bahama Purple, Black and Turquoise)
Flat and round paintbrushes
½" stencil paintbrush
Exterior acrylic finish

ENLARGE patterns, left, for 14" x 16" or 17" x 20" bunnies, or to desired size (see *How to Enlarge Patterns,* page 144).

CUT from wood. Glue and nail pieces together. Cut and center a supportive triangular brace or a stake at lower center back.

PAINT bunnies at least 2 coats white and egg a different color. Let dry. Add details as in photo. With stencil brush, stipple very dry purple lightly on tail. Apply finish.

EGG GARLAND

Colored scrapbook paper
Paper cut-outs in assorted shapes
Raffia
Tacky glue
Clear cellophane tape

CUT out egg shapes from colored scrapbook paper.

DECORATE with glued-on paper cutouts.

GLUE raffia to the back of eggs to join them together. Reinforce the glue with tape.

TIE a raffia bow between each egg.

Each square = 2" for small or 2½" for large

BUNNY BONNET ❶

*Fun Foam sheets in white, pink, dark pink,
    yellow and purple*
14" (or other size) straw hat
Wire or string for hanging
*Acrylic paints (we used Delta Ceramcoat
    White, Turquoise, Luscious Lemon, Pink
    Parfait, Bahama Purple and Black)*
Two 1" foam brushes
#8 round brush
¼" and ½" stencil paintbrushes
Low-temp glue gun
*Buttons: 2 each ½" maroon (for eyes) and ¾" white
    (for vest)*
Small amount of raffia

ENLARGE patterns, right (see *How to Enlarge Patterns*,
page 144). Cut from foam sheets, referring to photo,
right, for colors.

POKE wire through brim near edge and twist loop for
hanging.

PAINT hat crown white, brim turquoise with foam
brushes. With ¼" stencil brush, stipple yellow stripes
on vest and pink lines to indicate toes on paws. With
#8 round brush, paint pink message, purple lines and
turquoise dots on egg. Paint black mouth. With ½"
stencil brush, dab on pink cheeks.

GLUE pink ear to each white ear, foam pieces to hat,
buttons to face and jacket. Add raffia bow under chin.

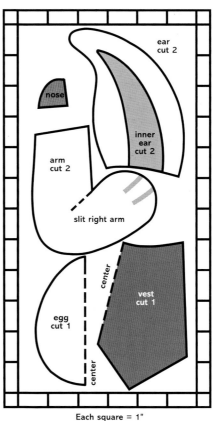

Each square = 1"

DECORATED EGGS ⓔ

These decorating techniques are safe for eggs that will be shelled and eaten.

*Hard-cooked eggs
Commercial Easter egg dye
Adhesive tape
Uni-Posca markers
Permanent adhesive stars, dots or reinforcement*

TIE-DYE (shown in photo, top left and center)

DIP egg briefly into dye to lightly color; let dry.

COVER sections of egg with pieces of tape. Press down edges with fingernail to be sure tape adheres.

DIP in second color dye; let dry. If you would like a third color, leave on tape but add smaller pieces. Dip in contrasting color. Dry and carefully remove tape.

DESIGNS (shown in photo, top, center, right)

COLOR eggs to desired shade, either light or dark; let dry.

MAKE swirls, stars or designs of your choice with markers.

APPLY permanent stickers to eggs.

DIP into dye of contrasting color; let dry, then remove stickers.

STRIPES (shown in photo, bottom right)

DYE egg a light color.

KEEP dipping egg into dye lengthwise, but submerge less and less egg each time.

PINK RABBIT

*45"-wide fabric: 1/2 yd pink, 1/2 yd polka-dot yellow,
1/4 yd polka-dot turquoise, 1/4 yd polka-dot green*
Thread to match fabrics
Fiberfill stuffing
6 chenille stems
Scrap of 8" x 10" thin white fabric or muslin
3 small buttons
Black dimensional paint
Embroidery thread in black and white
15" of 1/4"-wide wire-edge white ribbon
Craft spectacles (optional)

ENLARGE and cut out patterns, right (see *How to Enlarge Patterns*, page 144). Cut bunny parts from pink fabric. With right sides together, stitch around bunny about 1/8" from edge, leaving 2 1/2" at bottom and top of head open. Turn right side out and stuff firmly. Stitch legs in pairs, leaving tops open. Turn; stuff. Stitch across tops. Insert tops in bottom opening. Turning in raw edges, sew bottom closed.

PLACE three 8" lengths of chenille stems side by side for each ear. Encase in a piece of muslin scrap, sewing up the long edge and across one end to keep the stems flat.

SEW each pair of pink ears, right sides together, leaving the bottoms open. Turn right side out, insert the casings of chenille stems and stitch bottoms closed. Insert ears about 1/2" in head opening. Stitch first to back side of opening (stitch twice to secure), then slip-stitch the front edge closed as invisibly as possible.

VEST: Cut fabric for each pattern piece, following the colors shown in the photo. Stitch vest pieces for 1 front with right sides together, 1/8" seam, stitch, leaving the shoulder seam and underarm side open. Turn right side out; press. Repeat for the other vest pieces. Pin seams at shoulders and sides; stitch to secure and press seams open. Put on vest and pin closed. Sew on three buttons.

PANTS: Cut 2 pieces using the pattern. With right sides facing, stitch the inner and outer legs. Turn right side out; hem waist and leg bottoms. Sew pants on bunny. Dot on eyes with black dimensional paint, following manufacturer's instructions. Make nose and whiskers with embroidery thread. Tie bow and tack to neck; add spectacles if desired.

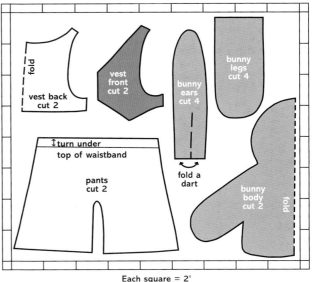

Each square = 2"

EASTER BONNETS ❶

Note: Materials listed are for all hats; if making only one or two, see individual instructions for supplies.

- *Sturdy white paper (bristol or posterboard)*
- *Drawing compass*
- *Adhesive dots*
- *Spray paints (we used Delta Color Mist Accents in yellow, fuchsia and turquoise)*
- *Wire-edged paper ribbon*
- *Pleated paper ribbon*
- *1 yd each assorted wide ribbons for ties (see instructions for each hat)*
- *Tissue Twist paper*
- *White paper mini-muffin cups*
- *Large (14") and small (12") paper doilies*
- *Spray glue*
- *Low-temp glue gun*
- *Stapler*
- *Tape*

BLUE DOTTED HAT

DRAW a 12½"-diameter circle of paper with compass; cut circle. Lightly press on adhesive dots in an even pattern; spray with turquoise paint, let dry and remove dots. In same manner, spray with fuchsia 2 yds of wire-edged paper ribbon.

GLUE pleated paper ribbon to outside edge.

GLUE on 2"-wide yellow satin ribbon in the center of the paper for ties.

MAKE paper flowers with Tissue Twist by cutting 4 pieces, laying them out, as shown on the diagram below, and stapling at center. Make muffin-cup flowers by grasping the center an shaping the paper. Staple 2 or 3 together. Mist flowers with color.

MAKE a large 10-loop bow.

GLUE bow and flowers to hat.

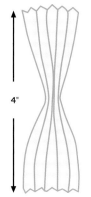

4"

PINK-STRIPED HAT

DRAW a 12½"-diameter circle of paper with compass; cut circle. Cut six 14" strips of paper 1½" wide. Place strips evenly across circle and secure with a bit of tape at each end.

SPRAY fuchsia stripes, let dry and remove paper strips.

SPRAY both sides of paper twist ribbon, 2 doilies and a muffin cup (see photo, opposite top right, for colors).

MAKE 2 large (about 6") paper twist bows; make a muffin-cup flower by grasping the center and shaping the paper.

CUT to center of a painted doily. Form fan by making 1" folds; repeat for second doily.

GLUE green 1½" satin ribbon for ties.

GLUE on fans, bows and flowers.

TULLE HAT

- *Yellow posterboard*
- *Plastic foam eggs*
- *Glitter paint*
- *2 yds of purple tulle*

DRAW a 12½"-diameter circle of yellow posterboard with compass; cut circle. Cut a 5½" hole in center.

CUT foam eggs in half.

PLACE eggs on newspaper cut side down; spray top surfaces with glue and dust with glitter.

GLUE egg halves all around hat brim.

PAINT on an edging of glitter with glitter paint.

CUT tulle into 12" width.

WRAP tulle around and around hat brim, knotting ends where they join.

DOILY HAT

DRAW a 12½"-diameter circle of paper with compass; cut circle.

PAINT large doilies yellow and purple; paint a smaller doily pink. Let dry.

GLUE (with spray glue) the yellow doily underneath the paper round and the purple doily on top; glue pink doily on top of the purple.

GLUE on flowered paper ribbon for ties.

MAKE flowers using 2 different size doilies. Glue over ribbon.

DESK ORGANIZER Ⓔ

Cereal box
Tacky glue (we used Aleene's Original)
Wrapping or decorative paper in assorted colors
Spraymount adhesive
Transparent and colored tape
Assorted cardboard food containers
Craft knife
Stickers

GLUE cereal box shut with tacky glue. Cut paper large enough to cover box. Spray box with adhesive; wrap and tape paper around box.

ARRANGE food containers as desired on side of cereal box; draw around shapes. Use craft knife to cut out.

CUT paper to cover sides of each container; spray with adhesive; wrap with paper.

INSERT covered containers into holes in box.

WORDY JOURNAL Ⓔ

Spiral journal
Sheet of heavyweight paper
Magazines
Tacky glue (we used Aleene's Original)
Clear Con-Tact paper

CUT heavyweight paper to fit front of journal. Glue in place.

CUT words and phrases from magazines; arrange and glue as desired on cover.

SEAL with Con-Tact paper, turning edges to inside.

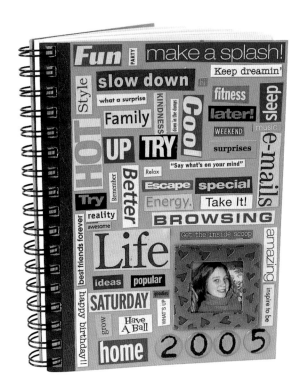

BOOKMARKS Ⓔ

Fun Foam in assorted colors
Decorative scissors (optional)
White glue
Fine-point permanent markers in assorted colors
¾" pompom
Two 5 mm movable eyes
Yarn

CUT 2" x 10" strips of Fun Foam for base of bookmark. Cut additional shapes, such as face or star. Use decorative scissors if desired.

GLUE shapes to one end of strip. Decorate shapes with markers, movable eyes, pompom nose, yarn and hair.

WRITE names of books you've read on base strip.

BOOK TREE Ⓔ

Construction paper: brown and assorted leaf colors
Tape
Low-temp glue gun
Twigs
Fine-point permanent markers in assorted colors

TAPE sheets of brown construction paper together. Draw and cut out tree shape.

GLUE twigs to tree trunk.

CUT leaf shapes from assorted colors of construction paper. Write title of book and author on a leaf for each one you've read.

GLUE leaves onto the tree, adding a new leaf after each book read.

POCKET IT

No more putting your pen in the spiral wire of your notebook and hoping it stays. Create a place for it on your notebook.

> Pocket from old pair of jeans or other piece of clothing
> Notebook with colorful cover
> Tacky glue (we used Aleene's Original)

CUT away small pocket from an old pair of jeans or other piece of clothing. (Leave the back, so the clothing stays intact.)

ATTACH pocket with tacky glue to the front of notebook. Let dry.

PORTFOLIO

> Construction paper in assorted colors
> Craft knife
> Large folder envelope
> Tacky glue (we used Aleene's Original)
> $\frac{1}{2}$"-wide ribbon

PLACE hands on colored paper and trace them with pencil. Repeat with different colored papers.

CUT them out and glue to envelope.

CUT two small openings on the top of the envelope.

SLIDE ribbon through slits to create closing.

PENCIL TOPPERS

> Fun Foam in assorted colors
> Craft knife
> Dimensional paint markers
> Pencils
> Hole punch

CUT out butterfly (or any flat shape) from foam, fold in half and cut two $\frac{1}{2}$" slits in center. Decorate with paint and slip over pencil.

CUT 3 different-sized circles for flower, and a pair of leaves; punch holes in centers. Snip "petals" into circle edges and arrange everything on pencil.

ANIMAL MAGNETS ⓔ

Precut wood shapes
Acrylic paints in assorted colors
Paintbrushes
Low-temp glue gun
Two 6 mm movable eyes
Chenille stem
2 magnets

PAINT precut wood shapes, use glue gun to form frog and butterfly. Let dry.

ADD movable eyes to frog and chenille-stem antennae to butterfly.

GLUE magnet to back to finish.

WATER BOTTLES ⓔ

Add some flavor to your water bottle.

Paint pens (metallic, glitter or dimensional)
Water bottle
Stickers (optional)
Charm on a ribbon (optional)
Sewing trim (optional)

USE paint pens to write inspirational messages or draw designs on the bottle. Be sure to allow time for ink to dry as you rotate it.

DECORATE the bottle with your favorite stickers.

HANG a charm on a ribbon or sewing trim and tie to bottle top, for more pizzazz.

NO-SKID SOCKS Ⓔ

Pair of socks
Cardboard, cut to foot size
Dimensional paint in assorted colors

WASH and dry a pair of socks.

STICK a piece of cardboard inside each sock to create a sturdy work surface.

USE dimensional paint to draw shapes and designs on bottoms.

LET the paint dry fully before wearing.

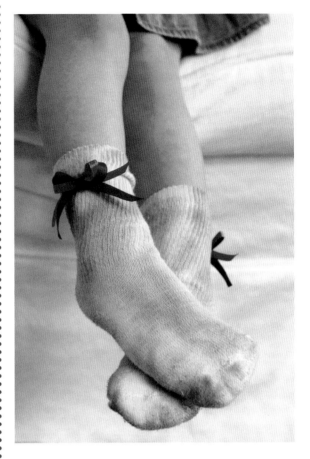

SOCK IT TO ME Ⓔ

Pair of cotton sport socks
Wax paper
Fabric paints in at least 2 colors (we used Tulip's Soft Brushable)
Brush
Bows and buttons
Washable fabric glue

WASH a pair of cotton sports socks and while still wet stuff each sock with crumpled wax paper.

DILUTE at least two colors of Tulip's Soft Brushable Fabric Paint with water.

BRUSH or drip thinned paint onto wet socks, one color at a time. Let dry.

ATTACH bows or buttons with washable fabric glue.

BEE LINE ⓔ

Buzz through spring with this button-up top.

> *Dark-color shirt*
> *Bee appliqué patch*
> *About twenty ⅜" white buttons*
> *Washable fabric glue*

GLUE a bee appliqué patch and buttons in a zigzag row across the front of a shirt, making sure to continue line across shirt fronts.

BUTTON COVERS ⓔ

Brighten up a plain shirt with these attention-getters.

> *Fun Foam in assorted colors*
> *Dimensional paints in assorted colors*

CUT shapes from colored Fun Foam and squiggle on bright dimensional paints as desired. Let dry.

CUT a slit in the center (matching the button width) and slip into place.

FLEECE SCARF 🅔

8"-wide strip of fleece in any color
Decorative scissors

CUT fleece strip to about 4 feet long (you may use a longer strip for an adult's scarf).

CUT 3"-deep fringe along both long edges of fleece.

BRACELET 🅔

Soft, clear plastic bottle
Sandpaper or emery board
Clear tape (optional)
Paper glue
Ribbon
Paper flowers, pompoms, sequins

CUT out a wide "bracelet" from a soft, clear plastic bottle and trim it to 1¼" wide.

MAKE 1 cut through the bracelet and trim ends so they are rounded and equal. The bracelet should be large enough to slip easily over a child's wrist.

SMOOTH all the edges with sandpaper or an emery board, or cover edges with clear tape.

GLUE a narrow piece of ribbon to the center of the bracelet, then glue colorful paper flowers and spirals on the ribbon and decorate them with pompoms and sequins.

STAR-SPANGLED  SNEAKERS

Compressed sponge
Royal blue soft brushable fabric paint
Canvas sneakers

CUT a small star shape from a compressed sponge.

SQUEEZE a small amount of blue fabric paint onto a plate.

DIP the star into the paint, dab off the excess and press it onto a canvas sneaker. Repeat until the sneaker is covered with stars.

STARRY TEE

White felt
Pins
Striped T-shirt
Red embroidery floss

CUT a large star from white felt and pin it to the front of a striped T-shirt.

SEW the star to the shirt with 3 strands of floss, using running stitches.

TIE off the ends on the inside of the shirt and remove pins.

HAT

Fun Foam sheets in assorted colors
Velcro Sticky Back Squares
Cap

CUT stars, bells or any shape you like from foam sheets.

SEPARATE hook and loop sections of Velcro Squares. Attach hook sections to backs of shapes. Attach loop sections randomly on cap.

FESTIVE BARRETTES ⓔ

Ribbon
Fabric glue
Barrettes
Woven or jelly jar label
Ribbon blossom or bows (optional)

GLUE barrette-length ribbon to the top of the barrette.

LOOP excess ribbon over the side of the barrette and glue underneath.

GLUE a woven or jelly label over the ribbon (we used labels from Making Memories).

ADD a blossom or bows for additional accents.

COLORFUL UMBRELLA ⓔ

Child-size umbrella
Chalk marking pencil
Paints for plastic in assorted colors
Paintbrush

OPEN umbrella. Lightly draw desired designs with chalk pencil on outside of umbrella.

PAINT designs with paint for plastic, letting base color dry before adding accents.

CUSTOMIZED PAIR ⓔ OF SHADES

Inexpensive pair of black sunglasses
Paints for plastic: yellow and red

PAINT red and yellow flames all over the frames.

LET each color dry before adding the next.

EYEGLASS CASE ⓔ

Sheet of Fun Foam
Hole punch
Plastic lacing
Acrylic paints in assorted colors
Velcro Sticky Back Squares

CUT a 4" x 4" square out of the upper left corner of an 8" x 12" piece of foam, then fold wide part from left to right.

PUNCH holes along 2 sides, as shown below, then join with plastic lacing. Print paint dots with your finger or a pencil eraser, then attach Sticky Back Squares to case and flap.

JINGLEBELL VEST

SIZE: *Chest: 28"; adjustable*

> ½ yd red fleece fabric
> 1 skein each red and green 6-strand
>   embroidery floss
> Embroidery needle
> Ribbons: ¾ yd of ⅜" green; 24" of ½"
>   patterned ribbon
> Washable fabric glue (we used Delta Stitchless)
>   or fusible web tape
> Six 16 mm green jingle bells
> Straight pins

ENLARGE patterns, below, ½" seam allowance included (see *How to Enlarge Patterns,* page 144). To make larger, add to sides, not armholes. To make smaller, decrease all sides, including armholes.)

CUT from fleece: 1 back on fold (blue line); 2 fronts (red line), reversing 1; 2 pockets.

PIN ½" back over front at sides and shoulders. Sew seams closed with a row of Xs, using 6 strands green floss. Blanket-stitch all edges with 6 strands red floss (see stitch diagram, right).

GLUE or fuse patterned ribbon crossed on pocket fronts, folding ½" ends over edges. Pin pockets to fronts, 1¼" from side and 1¾" from lower edge. Sew green-floss running stitch around pocket, attaching sides and bottom. Cut green ribbon in half; tie bows; sew or glue to pockets. Sew 3 bells ⅝" from each front edge.

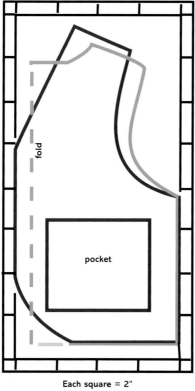

Each square = 2"

MITTEN-SCARF SET Ⓓ

54"-wide fleece fabric: ¾ yd medium blue (B),
⅓ yd royal blue (R), ⅙ yd each pale blue (P)
and teal (T)
6-strand embroidery floss: 1 skein white, 2 red
Embroidery needle
20 white buttons: eighteen ⅜" and two ½"
Blue thread
Straight pins, small safety pin

ENLARGE hat pattern below (see *How to Enlarge Patterns*, page 144). Hat with ⅝" seam fits 23" head; adjust size as needed.

HAT: Cut 2 each from B and R. With right sides together, stitch hats in pairs of same color, leaving bottoms open. Clip seams. Turn R right side out. Cut 6 each 2" squares P and 1½" squares T for appliqué. Embroidery: With red floss, center and whipstitch T to each P. With white, make straight-stitch snowflake tipped with French knots (see stitch diagram, right). Sew button to center with red. With white, whipstitch patches evenly spaced ½" from edge of B. Work red French knot centered between patches. Blanket-stitch around lower edge of hat (see stitch diagram, right). Turn up cuff. Pompom (optional): Cut 20½" x 5" strips each in 2 colors fleece. Stack, mixing colors; tie tightly at center. Trim. Fluff and pin to hat. Remove when reversing hat.

SCARF: For pattern, trace generous mitten shape around hand, making cuff 5¼" wide. Pin pattern to B fabric horizontally, with tip at side edge. Cut around mitten but extend length above cuff to 43" for half scarf. Turn pattern over and repeat. With mittens matching, sew scarf ends together. Stitch seam allowances down.

MITTENS: Cut 2 mitten shapes from R, reversing 1. From P, cut two 2" x 5¼" cuffs and 3½" squares (diamonds). Appliqué with squares and triangles of B and T, using red whipstitches. Embroider snowflakes and add buttons. Sew cuffs to R mittens with white whipstitches.

FINISHING: Pin R mittens to B mittens on scarf, right sides out. With white floss, blanket-stitch entire edge, attaching mittens.

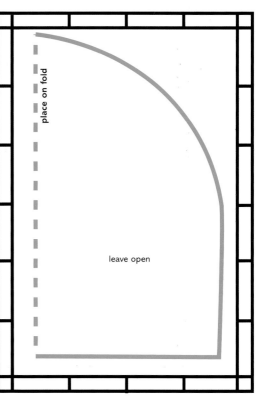

place on fold

leave open

Each square = 2"

FLOWERPOT PHOTO HOLDER Ⓔ

FOR EACH ONE

5"–7" x ¼"-diam dowel
2" wooden heart
Acrylic paints: red and green
Paintbrushes
2"–3" terra-cotta pot
Scraps of green craft paper, floral foam
  and basket grass
Low-temp glue gun
¾" binder clip

PAINT dowel green, heart red. Paint pot if you like.

CUT two 3"-long green leaves from craft paper.

GLUE clip with prongs unfolded and clip upward to back of heart near top to hold snapshot. Glue dowel below clip (it will cover one prong). Glue leaves to dowel.

FILL pot with foam and top with grass. Insert flower. Catch photo in clip.

FUNNY FRAME ⓔ

White glue
Plastic jar lid
Drinking straw
Chenille stems
Fun Foam sheets in assorted colors
2 black beads

GLUE a photo to a jar lid.

CUT a straw in half and glue to the back of the lid to make legs.

PUT chenille stems in straws and curl the ends to form feet.

CUT 2 small triangles and 2 small ovals out of Fun Foam.

GLUE triangles to the back of the lid for ears.

GLUE ovals above photo and add black beads to make eyes.

PUZZLE PICTURE ⓔ FRAME

Puzzle pieces
Acrylic paints in assorted colors
Paintbrushes
Wide-edge flat photo frame
Tacky glue

PAINT puzzle pieces a variety of colors.

DAB on dots of contrasting paint for a polka-dot effect. Let dry.

GLUE puzzle pieces to frame.

HOME-AND-FAMILY ❶ PORTRAIT

In a pinch, you could make this delightful home-and-family portrait with construction paper, but the Fun Foam adds an extra dimension. Give grandparents the place of honor on the second floor and let children fill the garden. Extra flowers can be for cousins or, perhaps, even a new delivery.

> *Assorted family photos*
> *Four each 12" x 18" red, purple, blue and yellow Fun Foam sheets*
> *Tacky glue*
> *17" square of foamcore board*
> *2 yds each striped ribbon and green rickrack*
> *Puffy paints: pink, green, orange and clear*
> *Package of precut felt animals and shapes*
> *White buttons, large red sequins, small colored and floral beads, pompoms*

TRIM photos for windows to 1⅜" squares; glue to 1¾" squares of yellow Fun Foam. Trim baby photos to 1¼" rounds.

CUT house (8½" x 11"), roof (11" x 3"), door (2" x 3¾"), chimney (1¼" x 2¼"), doghouse (2" x 3"), red triangle (2½" at base), 2 strips for doghouse roof and a round yellow sun from Fun Foam, matching colors as shown.

GLUE house to board 2½" above base and 2" from right edge, then glue on everything else. Use puff paint to make sun rays, dotted picture frames and stalks for bead flowers.

MEALTIME MEMORIES PLACEMAT Ⓔ

*Construction paper of contrasting colors
    and patterns
Paper glue
12" x 16" piece of card stock
Assorted photos or drawings
Clear Con-Tact paper*

CUT six 4" paper squares of contrasting colors and patterns.

GLUE onto card stock, alternating colors.

CUT smaller squares of paper in assorted colors and glue diagonally to centers of 4" squares.

GLUE pictures or drawings to each small square. Let dry.

COVER with Con-Tact paper.

LEAFY PLACEMATS Ⓔ

*Construction paper or felt in assorted colors
Fabric glue
Clear Con-Tact paper (optional)*

TRACE or draw a leaf onto paper and cut out to use as a pattern.

TRACE leaf shape onto colored felt or construction paper (you'll need about 12 leaves).

ARRANGE into a rectangle so that the leaves overlap each other with open spaces between them.

GLUE leaves together where they overlap. If using construction paper, protect with Con-Tact paper or laminate.

HANDY HOLDER Ⓔ

Scrap of wallpaper or gift wrap
Ruler
Two 9" foam plates
Tacky glue
Hole punch
2 yds of ½"-wide ribbon

TRACE around child's hand on scrap paper, adding 1" beyond wrist. Cut out hand shape.

MEASURE ¼ of the way down one foam plate. Using ruler, draw line straight across. Cut. Apply glue along edges of remaining ¾ plate and place facedown on top of second plate, forming a pocket. Press firmly. Let dry.

PUNCH a hole for ribbon hanger on either side of plate.

CUT ribbon in half. Thread an end of each ribbon into both holes. Tie ribbons together in a knot, leaving 1½" at ends.

GLUE paper hand to front of pocket. Slip a snapshot between fingers before glue dries.

A JAR FULL OF LOVE Ⓔ

Small glass jar with lid
Photograph
Double-stick tape
Candy hearts
8"-square of fabric
Rubberband
½ yd of ½"-wide ribbon

SOAK jar to remove label; wash and dry thoroughly.

TAPE photo inside jar. Fill with candy.

PLACE lid on jar. Center fabric on lid; secure with rubberband. Tie ribbon in bow over rubberband.

TWIGGY TICKER ⓔ

*Never lose track of time with this clock that
Mother Nature would approve of.*

> Cardboard
> Tacky glue
> Colored paper (optional)
> Colored paint (optional)
> Craft knife
> Clock set (available at crafts stores)
> Hole punch
> Leaves, twigs, dried flowers, bark

TRACE a cardboard circle with a plate as your guide
for the face.

GLUE on colored paper or paint cardboard.

CUT an "X" in the middle and punch out a hole for the
clock shaft.

GLUE on leaves, twigs, dried flowers, etc. Glue bark
onto clock hands, making sure you leave enough room
for them to move.

SPRING BIRD ⓔ

> Two 9" paper plates
> Craft knife
> Sheet of decorative paper
> Tacky glue (we used Aleene's Original)
> Stickers or black fine-point permanent marker

FOLD one plate in half. Cut a 4½" slit on each side to
hold wings (A); cut a 1¼" slit in the back to hold tail
(B).

CUT second plate in half. Trim one of the halves by
1" along its straight edge. Slip into the first plate for
wings.

TRIM the second half by 1" along its straight edge,
then cut in half. Use one of the pieces for the tail.

CUT a triangle from decorative paper, then fold it in half
for a beak. Glue it to the underside of the plate, at the
opposite end from the tail.

USE stickers or a marker for eyes.

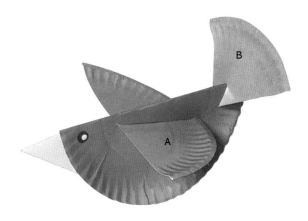

VICTORIAN CARD

Parchment or construction paper
Craft knife
Pinking shears
Colored paper and magazines for cutouts
Glue stick or rubber cement

TRACE your hand on paper and draw a 3"-long triangular cuff at the wrist. Cut out with craft knife; trim cuff with pinking shears.

CUT a 1½" x 2" heart from folded colored paper with pinking shears. Leave heart folded and fold it again diagonally; snip about 1" at center of diagonal fold with pinking shears. Glue to hand cutout.

PENCIL 2 bands across back, one ½" wide just below palm and the other ⅝" wide, near lower edge. Cut a row of X's along each band, leaving a tiny space between X's at top and bottom. Slip a strip of paper through each band, leaving diamonds showing between X's on front. Cut wedge in ends of strips.

PRINT message across cuff.

BRIGHT HEARTS CARD

Parchment or construction paper
Colored paper and magazines for cutouts
Craft knife
Glue stick or rubber cement

CUT 5 hearts the same size from different colors of construction paper. Fold in half.

CUT varied letters and words from colored paper and magazines to spell out a 5-word message.

GLUE 1 word inside each heart. Tape hearts in a row at back edges.

SNIPPED CARD

Red rice paper
Sharp scissors
Metallic gold fine-point marker

CUT an 8"-diam circle of red rice paper and fold it precisely into 16ths (fold in half 4 times).

DRAW a half-heart pattern on top for snipping, leaving some folds intact on each side.

CUT out design with scissors.

OPEN paper and write message in gold marker around the circle. Refold on original creases for neat results.

HIDDEN-HEART CARD

Sturdy colored paper: 5" x 10" blue and
*   4"-square red*
Tracing paper
Craft knife
Glue stick or white glue
Fine-point permanent marker

FOLD blue paper in half to form square, then unfold.

TRACE blue heart and cut out tracing. Outline heart on center front of card, marking left edge between dots as "hinge."

CUT out heart with craft knife, leaving hinge.

GLUE red paper behind opening. Glue blue card closed. Fold back blue heart; write message on red one; close.

CURLICUE CARD ⓔ

Colored construction paper
Craft knife
Paper glue
Colored cardboard

CUT colored construction paper into ¼" strips. Roll the strips into round shapes.

GLUE the end of each strip to its roll so it doesn't unwind.

ARRANGE the shapes on a piece of colored cardboard as desired and glue into place.

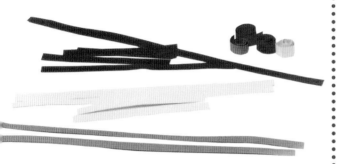

SPRING GREETINGS ⓔ

Show Mom how much you love her with a pot of flowers she won't have to water.

Light-color construction paper
Card stock
Craft knife
Green and assorted colors construction paper
Glue stick
Fine-point permanent marker

FOLD sheet of construction paper in half to make a card.

CUT flowerpot shape from card stock and glue edges (except top) to front of card.

CUT stems from green construction paper and petals from assorted colored papers.

GLUE stems to flowers and, when dry, write notes to Mom on each stem.

PUT flowers in vase to complete.

LIGHTHOUSE Ⓓ
BIRDHOUSE

2-ft length of 1 x 12 pine
Saber saw
Tapered 9½"-high metal flower bucket 6" wide at top
Drawing compass
Wood glue and household "Goop" glue
1" nails
Hammer
Coarse- and medium-grade sandpaper
2" length of 1½" dowel
5" plastic funnel
Drill
3" flathead wood screw
Screwdriver
1" wooden knob or bead
4" x 4½" x 4½" unpainted wooden birdhouse
White spray primer
Acrylic paints (we used FolkArt Sunny Yellow, Azure Blue, Indigo, Calico Red and Medium Gray)
Flat paintbrushes
Clear protective finish

SAW a 10" length of 1 x 12 pine for project base.

REMOVE bucket handles by bending them off slowly or by sawing away bolts.

CUT one 5"-diam circle and four 3½"-diam circles for lighthouse window area using compass. With wood glue and nails, attach one 3½" circle to center of 5" circle. Stack, glue and nail remaining 3½" circles on top of the first 3½" circle. Smooth sides with rough, then medium sandpaper.

GLUE 1½" dowel to center top of 3½" circles. Let dry.

SAW off funnel tip leaving ½" attached. Place funnel upside down over the dowel, for roof. Drill pilot hole for 3" screw through 1" wooden knob and dowel and screw knob over funnel tip.

PLACE lighthouse and birdhouse, side by side diagonally on base. In a well-ventilated area, glue with Goop.

PRIME entire piece. Let dry.

PAINT following photo for colors. Let dry.

SAND edges and surface for aged look. Apply clear finish. Let finish cure for 2 weeks before placing outside.

BIRDHOUSE Ⓓ

SIZE: *6" w x 8¾" d x 8½" h (plus 3" steeple) on 8½" x 12" base.*

- *½"-thick pine: two 5½" x 9" (house front and back), two 5½" x 7¼" (sides), 12" x 8½" (base)*
- *Saber saw*
- *Drill with ¼" bit*
- *¼"-thick plywood: 1 each 10" x 5" and 10" x 5³⁄₁₆" (roof)*
- *Steel square (optional)*
- *Scraps of plywood or 18" of 5¼" x ¼" lattice (door and window trims)*
- *1" brads*
- *Solid wood for steeple and steeple roof (see diagram, right)*
- *Wood glue*
- *3" x ¼"-diam dowel*
- *Wood primer*
- *Water-based exterior or acrylic paints: red, white, green, blue and gold*
- *Masking tape*
- *1½" finishing nails*
- *Hammer*
- *Sandpaper*
- *Wood putty*
- *Nail set*
- *Screwdriver*
- *Four 1½" screws*

NOTE: *To assemble birdhouse, glue and nail pieces together. Set all nails. Fill holes with putty. Sand smooth.*

FRONT AND BACK: Cut peaks, following diagram, right, centering corner of square at top to mark angle. Cut bird hole and drill perch hole in front.

SIDES: Assemble between front and back with outer edges flush.

BASE: Set house 1¾" in from front edge of base. Mark position. Predrill holes for screws through base into house corners, so you can unscrew to clean. Install after painting.

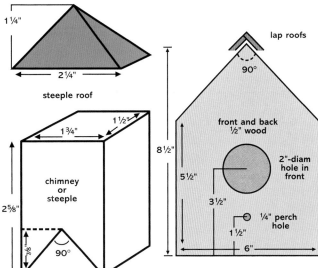

ROOF: Center pieces on house top with even overhang at each end; lap wider over narrower piece at peak (see detail).

TRIMS: Trace orange and green patterns, left. Cut from ¼" wood, making 2 for side windows. (Check holes against front before cutting door trim.) Glue in position and tack with brads, centering a window on each long side ½" from bottom and placing diamond window ½" above door trim.

GLUE dowel into perch hole.

CHIMNEY OR STEEPLE: Cut pieces following diagram, above. Install after painting.

PRIME AND PAINT pieces, masking edges of details. Paint red and green diamonds inside window openings; add gold borders to colors.

FINISHING: Nail steeple roof to steeple and steeple (or chimney) to roof, 2" in from front edge. Screw house to base.

BIRDBATH ⓘ

Old crockery and/or tiles, including blue, white and yellow for bird, greens and floral prints for background
Hammer
14"-diam terra-cotta flowerpot saucer
Tile nippers
1 pt white or tinted acrylic tile grout (or black acrylic paint to tint grout)
Spatula or spackling knife

WRAP crockery and tiles in a paper bag or cloth and break them with a hammer.

LAY shards on newspaper next to clay saucer and plan design. Refine any shapes with the nippers.

MIX paint little by little into grout until color is pale gray.

SPREAD grout on inside of saucer with spatula, making layer thick enough to hold and squeeze up between tiles. Starting in center, press tiles into the grout, leaving ⅛"–¼" spaces between them. Wipe rim of saucer clean. Let grout dry.

PICKET BIRD FEEDER ⓘ

Three 10½" x 7" premade picket fences or 18 ft of ¼" x 1½" lattice strips to build fences
9" x 10¼" piece of ½"-thick plywood for floor
Acrylic paints (we used Accent's blue, red, green and Adobe Wash and Plaid's FolkArt Azure Blue, Tangerine, Poppy Red, Shamrock and Periwinkle for cutouts)
Paintbrushes
Sandpaper
White primer (optional)
About 8 wooden gardening-themed cutouts
Brads
1½" galvanized nails
Clear exterior varnish
2 black-painted metal 9" x 10½" brackets with four ½" screws
4 screws and anchors for wall

NAIL assembled fences to two 10¼" and one 9" side of plywood, trimming ends to fit neatly at corners as needed.

PAINT fence and brackets off-white (Adobe Wash) and floor green. When dry, sand fence to reveal undercolor.

APPLY white primer or paint as undercoat on cutouts. Paint cutouts, let dry and nail to fence with brads. Apply clear finish.

SCREW brackets to bottom, and to wall using anchors.

SUMMER FLAG 🄸

¾ yd 54"-wide Waverly ⅜"-checked blue gingham
Fabric scraps for appliqués: blue and red
Letters from typebook, newspaper or stencil to
*   enlarge for names*
Pellon lightweight Wonder-Under transfer web
Dimensional fabric paints: red, navy and white

CUT gingham fabric 20" x 28" for flag. Cut five 2" x 18" bias or straight strips for ties.

TURN under ¼" twice on edges of background; top-stitch. Fold each tie lengthwise, wrong side out; seam ⅛" in from long edges. Turn right side out; press.

ENLARGE bird, right (see *How to Enlarge Patterns*, page 144). Photocopy letters for names, and make them 3½" high (or whatever size is needed for names to fit on flag).

TRACE letter and bird appliqué patterns. Apply Wonder-Under to back of appliqué fabric scraps, following manufacturer's directions and photo. Leave paper backing on. Trace designs onto paper reversed, and cut out. Arrange and iron onto flag, following manufacturer's directions. (Rows of checks on flag are good guidelines for base of letters.)

APPLY a line of paint on raw edges of appliqués, starting at top. When dry, outline birds' wings inside bodies with a contrasting color and make dot for eyes. Let dry.

STITCH center of ties to back at left-side corners and evenly spaced between.

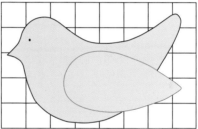

Each square = 1"

CUSTOM BALL 🄴

Never lose your toys at the playground again.

*   Rubber softball or larger ball*
*   Dimensional paint pens and glitter paint pens*
*   in assorted colors*
*   Plastic or paper cup*

DRAW your design on ball with pencil.

PLACE ball in cup to hold it while you paint designs. Let dry, then turn ball to paint other side.

PINWHEEL ❶

8" square each red, white and blue medium-weight paper
Craft knife
White glue
Blue acrylic paint
16" length of ⅛" or ¼" dowel
Spray adhesive
Ball-head straight pin

MARK diagonals on red paper lightly with pencil, following diagram, left.

CUT away large right-hand triangle of blue, but leave the ¾"-wide red section at center right ("X" on diagram) so you can glue it back.

CUT blue to fit entire missing triangle. Fit blue in place and glue to red "X" section with white glue; weight and let dry.

PAINT dowel.

CUT four 1" x 9" strips white paper. Attach with spray adhesive, trimming to fit as shown.

TRACE and cut a star. Glue in place.

CUT slit from red corners in, ending ¾" before center.

PLACE design facedown and mark center with a dot. Curl points to center and pierce with pin, then press pin through at dot and firmly into dowel. (Premake hole in dowel with a pushpin or a fine drill bit if necessary.)

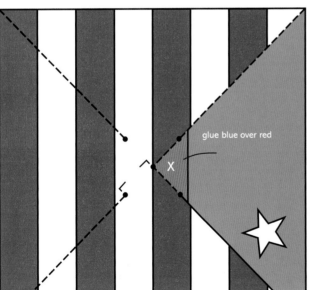

glue blue over red

X

FISH KITE ❶

*Tissue paper: 20" x 26" sheet of yellow to decorate
for body (optional: green and pink for gills and
eyes, scrap dark blue for pupils)*

*Fine-point permanent markers, crayons or stamps,
or green and orange liquid food coloring to dye
stripes as shown*

*1" x 20" strip of posterboard or other bendable,
sturdy cardboard*

Stapler

White glue

Single hole punch

Ball of thin cord

FOLD tissue paper for the body in half lengthwise to
be 10" x 26".

TO DECORATE: Draw gills at top and fins 12" below
on each side with markers or crayon and decorate the
fish as you like. (Note: If you prefer to make the kite
look more like the photograph, follow directions for
dyeing paper and gluing on gills and fins, below.)

OVERLAP ends of 20" cardboard strip 1" and staple to
form a 19" ring for the bridle (fish's mouth).

GLUE top end of fish's body to outside of ring. Overlap
1" at sides of paper and glue closed. Cut curves in tail
leaving total length about 25".

PUNCH 4 evenly spaced holes in the ring (1 every
4¾").

TIE a 12" string in each hole. Tie the ends together so
each string is 7" long when joined at the center. Trim
excess string. Tie, then wrap more string around a stick
or strip of stiff cardboard and tie the end where strings
join on the bridle, so you can fly the kite.

TO DYE THE PAPER:

FOLD the 10" x 26" folded paper back and forth
lengthwise in accordion folds to form a strip about
2" x 26".

ACCORDION-FOLD strip up in 4½" lengths to be
2" x 4½".

MIX 4 drops food coloring with 3 tablespoons water in
a saucer. Spread out newspapers for drying.

DIP only the very corners at one end of the packet in
orange dye and lift it out quickly so you don't soak the
paper. The color will spread.

DIP the opposite corners in green dye.

UNFOLD the paper very carefully, touching only the dry
places. (Wet paper tears easily, so it's a good idea to
dye a few extra sheets.) Lay it on newspapers to dry.
(If paper needs to be smoothed when dry, iron it under

a sheet of paper on a low
heat setting.)

**TO ADD GILLS, SINS
AND EYES:** Cut 2 gills, 4
fins (2 pink and 2 green)
and 2 eyes and pupils from
paper. Diagrams, above,
show suggested sizes; if
you want to be exact, copy
the patterns on graph
paper. Glue pupils to eyes.
When dry, glue 1 eye to
center of each gill.

CONTINUE with last 3
steps of kite directions.
Glue gills and fins in place
after attaching the body.

gill

7"

9½"

3"

fin

7"

6"

3"

eye

UNCLE SAM 🅔 CENTERPIECE

Gallon water or milk jug
Craft knife
Acrylic paints: white, red and blue
Paintbrushes
9" foamcore or cardboard disk
Can or oatmeal box
Low-temp glue gun
Black fine-point permanent marker
Cotton batting

CUT a big mouth (3" x 5") in a gallon water or milk jug.

PAINT blue background on foamcore or cardboard disk. Let dry. Paint white stars on disk.

PAINT red and white stripes on can or oatmeal box.

GLUE disk to top of gallon water or milk jug, then glue can or oatmeal box to top of disk.

PAINT face and hat with marker, let dry.

USE batting for beard and brows. Glue to face.

WIND CLICKER 🅔

2¼" x 5" terra-cotta pot
Drill
4"-wide wooden stars
Acrylic paints: white, red and blue
Paintbrush
Hanging loop
Red pearls
String

DRILL 3 holes at the bottom of the pot and in wooden stars as shown on photo.

PAINT and let dry. Add hanging loop and red pearls as shown on photo. String stars to dangle and touch when the wind blows.

FOURTH OF JULY 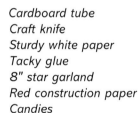 "FIRECRACKERS"

Tacky glue
Fun Foam
Cardboard tube
Beads, beans and paperclips
Ribbons, stars and confetti

GLUE Fun Foam around a cardboard tube.

CUT 2 foam circles and glue 1 over 1 end of the tube.

PUT some beads, beans or paperclips inside the tube, then glue the other circle over the open end.

DECORATE with colorful ribbons, stars and confetti.

FIRECRACKER FAVOR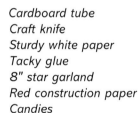

Cardboard tube
Craft knife
Sturdy white paper
Tacky glue
8" star garland
Red construction paper
Candies

TRACE ends of a cardboard tube and cut from white paper.

GLUE 1 circle to bottom.

GLUE "wick" of garland into circle for lid.

WRAP tube in red paper.

FILL with candies; place lid on top.

LEAPFROG ⓔ HOPSCOTCH

Sheets of green, black, white, pink and yellow
  Fun Foam
Tacky glue (we used Aleene's Original)
Black medium-point permanent marker

CUT 4 frog shapes and 8 arms from sheets of green Fun Foam, making each frog about 10" high.

CUT out eyes from black and white foam, and glue all parts to frogs.

USE a black marker to draw a mouth.

CUT 6 lily pads from green foam, and 3 flowers each from pink and yellow foam.

GLUE flowers to lily pads. Number with marker, and hip hop away!

RHYTHM BLOCKS

12" of 2" x 4" wood
Handsaw
Acrylic paints in assorted colors
Dimensional paints in assorted colors
Paintbrushes
Coarse sandpaper
Tacky glue (we used Aleene's Original)

CUT two 6" pieces from wood. Sand edges.

PAINT all but one side of rhythm blocks and accent with dimensional paint. Cut coarse sandpaper to fit block fronts.

GLUE on and weight with a book to dry.

RAIN STICK

Heavy paper in assorted colors
Cardboard gift-wrap tube
Masking tape
1 cup of uncooked rice
Scraps of felt
2 small buttons
Feathers
Chenille stems
Tacky glue (we used Aleene's Original)

TWIST a long strip of heavy paper into a spiral, drop into a cardboard gift-wrap tube and tape ends to tube.

COVER one end of the rain stick with tape, pour in a cup of rice and close other end with tape.

WRAP with strips of colored paper, add a folded-heart "beak," felt and button eyes, feathers, chenille stems. Secure with tape or glue.

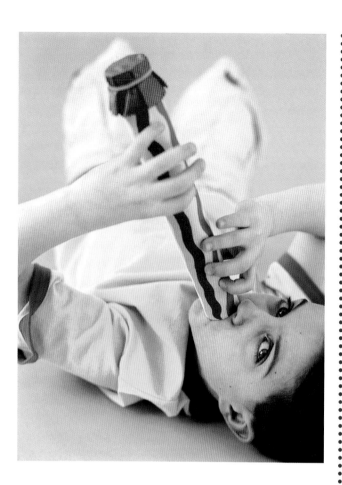

TOOT YOUR HORN Ⓔ

Lead the "charge" cheer.

>   Cardboard paper towel tube
>   Screwdriver
>   Acrylic paints in assorted colors
>   Paintbrush
>   Tissue paper
>   Rubberband

PUNCH 4 holes in a cardboard paper towel tube using a screwdriver.

ENLARGE the last hole with a pencil.

PAINT the entire tube a solid color, then once it's dry, add a design with other colored paints.

STACK 3 pieces of tissue paper and cut out a circle about 4" in diameter.

COVER the end of the tube with tissue paper circles and secure with a rubberband.

TAMBOURINE MAN Ⓔ

Keep the beat with this funny-face instrument.

>   2 paper plates
>   Hole punch
>   Ribbon
>   Bells
>   Tacky glue
>   Chenille stems
>   2 movable eyes in different sizes

GLUE the paper plates together.

PUNCH holes around the edge about 1" apart.

THREAD a ribbon through the holes, threading on a bell at every other hole.

GLUE on a face using chenille stems and movable eyes.

PARTY PINWHEELS ⓔ

FOR EACH ONE

Striped or dotted paper
Straight pin
2 small beads
Thread
Pencil eraser

CUT and fold a 6"- to 8"-square of paper on a diagonal, corner to corner. Then fold in half, matching small corners.

UNFOLD completely and cut along each fold two-thirds of the way to the center, creating 8 points.

FOLD every other point to the center. Stick a pin through these 4 points and the center of paper.

THREAD 2 small beads onto the pin and stick the end into the side of a pencil's eraser.

PARTY FAVOR FRAME ⓔ

FOR EACH ONE

Cutting board or scrap matboard
Craft knife
Ruler
4" x 5" green felt sheet and two ³⁄₄" x 7" strips
  white, or desired colors
Pinking shears
White glue
Wave fabric shears (Fiskars)
Four ³⁄₈" buttons or glue-on jewels
2 pieces of thin, stiff matboard for backing: 3" x 4"
  and 2" x 3"
2" x 3" photo or copy
Plastic or paper adhesive tape

SCORE and cut a 1³⁄₄" x 1¹⁄₂" opening in center of larger matboard piece, guiding knife along straightedge.

TRIM 4" x 5" felt with pinking shears, to about 3³⁄₈" x 4³⁄₈". Center and glue matboard frame on back. Cut an "X" in felt at frame opening from corner to corner (start with knife; cut with scissors). Trim cut flaps to ⁵⁄₈"-wide; glue to back.

CUT two 3¹⁄₂" and two 2³⁄₄" white felt strips. Trim 1 side of each with wave or pinking shears, making strips about ¹⁄₂" wide and matching waves at ends. Place around front opening with ends overlapped. Cut from outer corner through both layers to miter and butt corners. Glue strips down. Glue buttons or jewels to corners. Let dry.

TAPE photo and smaller board to back.

INVITATIONS

Photocopy the invitations, add some color and send them to your friends!

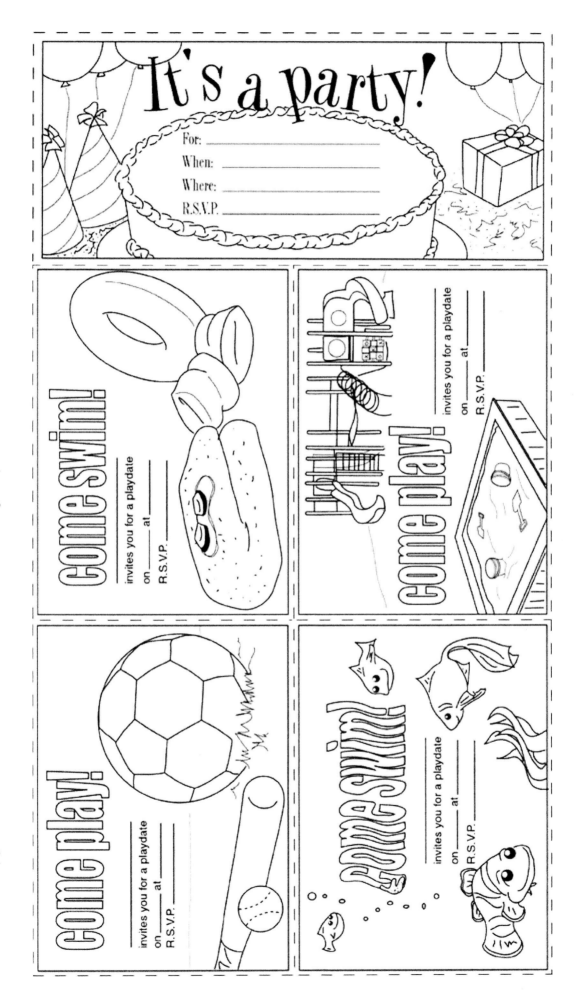

It's a party!

For: _____
When: _____
Where: _____
R.S.V.P. _____

come swim!

invites you for a playdate
on _____ at _____
R.S.V.P. _____

come play!

invites you for a playdate
on _____ at _____
R.S.V.P. _____

come play!

invites you for a playdate
on _____ at _____
R.S.V.P. _____

come swim!

invites you for a playdate
on _____ at _____
R.S.V.P. _____

TRENDY TACKS 🇪

Magazine (optional)
Small ceramic tiles
Tacky glue (we used Aleene's Original)
Movable eyes (optional)
Pompoms (optional)
Yarn (optional)

CUT out letters or pictures from magazines, or draw your own designs on small squares of paper, and glue onto small ceramic tiles. Or create faces on the tiles by gluing on movable eyes, a pompom nose and yarn hair and adding a puff-paint mouth.

GLUE a tack onto the back of each tile and let dry.

UNDER THE SEA 🇪

You'll never have to fish around for important papers again with this ocean-themed bulletin board.

Framed corkboard
Acrylic paints: blue and green
Paintbrush
Tacky glue
Shells and small stones
Fun Foam in assorted colors
Markers (optional)
Pushpin tops

PAINT the framed corkboard with 2 coats of blue paint. Let dry, then paint on green seaweed.

ATTACH shells and small stones to the bottom of the board with tacky glue.

CUT out fish shapes from craft foam (or use precut shapes and decorate with markers), and glue shapes to pushpin tops.

DOORKNOB MESSAGE CENTER (E)

Paper pad
Foamies Door Hanger
Beads, charms or small toys
Pencil with elastic cord or craft wire
Ribbon

GLUE a paper pad onto a Foamies Door Hanger.

GLUE on beads, charms or small toys for decoration.

ATTACH a pencil with elastic cord or craft wire.

ADD ribbon streamers: poke holes through the bottom of the hanger, push ribbon through and tie beads to the ends.

MESSAGE BOARD (E)

Keep track of dates and events with a personal message board you can update in an instant.

Frame or plywood rectangle with photo cutout
Sandpaper
Green or black Krylon Chalk Board Paint
Photograph
Ribbon
Tacky glue (we used Aleene's Original)

START with a purchased frame or a plywood rectangle with photo cutout.

SAND and seal the frame, then apply at least 2 coats of Chalk Board Paint (your choice of green or black) following the manufacturer's instructions.

INSERT photo, glue ribbon around edges and decorate with dotted borders (we used cotton swabs to dab on paint).

BIRDS ON THE WING

When the real things have flown south, it's especially nice to have this bright, cheery flock bouncing around the house.

- *12" x 18" sheets of orange, yellow and purple Fun Foam*
- *Hole punch*
- *Feathers: red and yellow*
- *Decorative sequins*
- *White glue*
- *Bright yarn*
- *Small tree branch*

ENLARGE patterns below (see *How to Enlarge Patterns*, page 144). Trace outlines on Fun Foam and cut out 4 of each. For each bird: Cut slit and punch hole in body as shown.

DECORATE by gluing on feathers, sequins and fancy feathers and collars cut from Fun Foam.

DAB glue on slit in body and slide wing in place; hold till glue sets.

KNOT yarn through hole and tie other end to branch. Hang indoors or out.

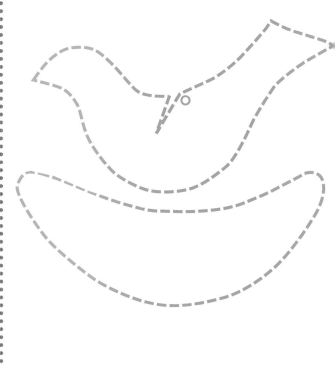

MOBILE Ⓔ

Various shapes of cookie cutters
Sheets of Fun Foam in each color shown in photo
Craft knife
Hole punch
White glue
2 craft sticks
Raffia

TRACE outlines of 5 cookie cutters onto foam sheets and cut out. (All cutouts should be similar in size.) Punch a hole in each cutout, then sponge lightly with white paint.

GLUE craft sticks together at right angles. Tie raffia to each cutout, and knot the other end around the craft sticks. Tie one cutout to the center. Balance the mobile by adjusting the lengths of the raffia if necessary, then glue in place on sticks. Tie on a loop of raffia for hanging.

BEAUTIFUL BUTTERFLIES Ⓔ

FOR EACH ONE

Two-ply paper towel
Watercolor or tempera paint
Paintbrush
Craft (or ice pop) stick
String
Tacky glue (we used Aleene's Original)
Narrow black ribbon or yarn

PAINT a white two-ply paper towel with colorful patterns using watercolor or tempera paint. Set aside to dry on a baking rack.

FOLD towel in half and cut out a butterfly wing shape. Unfold and trim the center top and bottom so that the center is the length of a craft (or ice pop) stick.

TIE a length of string around the middle of a craft stick. Align the stick with the center of wings; glue in place. Flip over: glue another stick to the underside of wings.

CUT a small length of thin black ribbon or yarn; tie a knot in the center. Glue to craft stick for antennae.

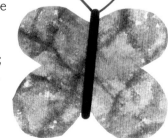

STRING LANTERNS

Thin cardboard
Tracing paper
Drawing compass
Colored vellum papers (we used Cromatica Extra
    White, Azure, Turquoise, Absinthe, Yellow,
    Vermilion and Canson Rose Text)
Assorted Fiskars paper edgers (pinking, wide pinking,
    seagull, Victorian and long scallop, majestic)
Assorted Fiskars punches (square, heart, star,
    1/16" hole)
String of small white lights
Double-sided clear tape

TRACE half-pattern, printed over text, placing broken line on fold. Cut pattern as template from cardboard. Cut 1 from vellum for each lightbulb.

DECORATE with edgers and punches.

WRAP 1 around each bulb and seal with tape folded in half lengthwise.

LAMPSHADE

Small fabric lampshade
Acrylic paints in assorted colors
Paintbrush

COAT a small fabric lampshade with a bright color of acrylic paint. Let dry.

ADD spots or stripes in a contrasting color, using paintbrush.

CARDBOARD CASTLE ❶

Cardboard box (any size)
Yardstick
Craft knife
Tempera paints: blue for the moat, another color for the castle
Paintbrush or sponge brush
Gold braid, yarn or string for drawbridge cable
Flat-backed craft jewels, pearls or sequins for decoration
Flat piece of cardboard (a few inches larger than the perimeter of the box)
10" wire-edged ribbon for flags
Low-temp glue gun or tacky glue
4 craft sticks or toothpicks
Clear tape

REMOVE and discard flaps from top of box.

ENLARGE pattern, right (see *How to Enlarge Patterns*, page 144). Use yardstick and pencil to sketch cutting lines on box (see figure A, right).

USE scissors and craft knife to cut notches into top of castle walls.

USE craft knife to cut open drawbridge door. Leave bottom of door attached to box.

PAINT castle (may need 2 coats) and let dry.

USE pencil to puncture 2 small holes above drawbridge and on the drawbridge door itself (see figure A, below).

THREAD braid, yarn or string through holes of drawbridge and knot ends (see figure B, below).

USE glue gun or tacky glue to attach jewels or other decorations.

PLACE castle on flat piece of cardboard. Sketch a curvy edge around perimeter. Trim excess, paint blue and let dry.

CUT ribbon into 4 even pieces. Glue 1 edge to craft stick or toothpick. Cut a V-shaped notch in the center of the other edge. Attach flag to inside of castle turrets with tape.

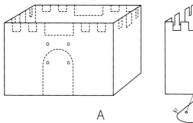

A

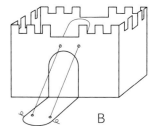

B

MONEY MONSTER ⓔ

This creature helps you save your pennies.

> *Clear mason jar*
> *Cardboard*
> *Scraps of felt*
> *Craft knife*
> *Tacky glue*
> *Trims*
> *Pompoms in assorted colors*
> *Fun Foam in assorted colors*
> *Chenille stems*
> *Two 15 mm movable eyes*

RINSE out a clear mason jar and trace a circle out of cardboard and felt for the lid.

GLUE felt to cardboard and cut a slit for a mouth.

SCREW back on with metal ring.

GLUE on trims, pompoms, Fun Foam, chenille stems and movable eyes to make a monster face.

BANK ON IT! ⓔ

Pigs aren't the only place to store your dimes. Why not put away your savings in this cute zebra-inspired bank?

> *Clear 16-oz water bottle*
> *Black Fun Foam*
> *Craft knife*
> *Acrylic paints: black and white*
> *Paintbrush*
> *Black and white yarn*
> *Tacky glue (we used Aleene's Original)*
> *Two 20 mm movable eyes*
> *4 empty thread spools*

COVER the body of water bottle with Fun Foam and cut a coin slot in the top.

PAINT white stripes on foam.

GLUE on black and white yarn for the mane and tail.

CUT black Fun Foam ears and attach with movable eyes.

PAINT 4 small empty thread spools black and glue to the underside of the bank.

IN THE POM OF ⓔ YOUR HAND

Why let socks and sweaters get all the attention? Make yarn come to life with these pom puppets.

FOR EACH ONE

Yarn
Cardboard
Two 10 mm movable eyes
Scraps of felt or paper
Feathers and sequins
Tacky glue (we used Aleene's Original)

WRAP yarn around a 2" to 3" piece of cardboard many times (the more you wrap the fuller the pompom).

PULL off and pinch in the middle, tightly wrapping 2 long strands of yarn around the center, and tie 2 knots.

CUT all loops and use the long strands to tie around the top of a pencil. Trim and fluff pompom. Add movable eyes and use felt or paper for ears and nose. Decorate with feathers and sequins.

SOCK PUPPET ⓔ

Give new life to an old sock by turning it into a puppet, like this cute caterpillar.

Clean sock
Two 25 mm movable eyes
Two 1" pompoms
1/2" pompom
Tacky glue (we used Aleene's Original)
Fun Foam scraps
1/2 yd of jumbo rickrack

PUT the sock on your hand to see where the eyes and mouth should go. Mark placement with pencil dots.

GLUE on a movable eye to each large pompom. Glue at eye marks. Glue small pompom below eyes for nose.

CUT long tongue from foam. Glue into mouth area.

CUT rickrack in half; glue to back for legs.

WINDOW DECOR Ⓔ

FOR EACH ONE

2 chenille stems
Colorful beads
Metallic paper in assorted sizes
Hole punch
Fishing line

TWIST the bottom halves of chenille stems together and string beads onto the twisted portion. Fold up the bottoms to secure the beads.

CUT slits in metallic paper to make the wings. Punch holes in the wings and string them onto chenille stems.

ADD a final bead and curl the top of the chenille stems to create the antennae. Use fishing line to hang.

THREE BUGS IN Ⓔ
A ROW

Put a twist on the classic game of tic-tac-toe.

White and green Fun Foam
Craft knife
Tacky glue (we used Aleene's Original)
Cardboard egg carton
Acrylic paints: red, yellow and black
Paintbrush
Eight 1" pompoms (4 red and 4 yellow)
Sixteen 10 mm movable eyes
Chenille stem
Ribbon or lace

CUT two 7½" squares from white and green Fun Foam.

DIVIDE the green piece into 9 equal squares and cut out.

GLUE 5 of the green squares to the large white square in an alternating pattern.

CUT and trim 8 cups from a cardboard egg carton.

PAINT 4 red and 4 yellow. When dry, add black dots.

GLUE on pompom heads and noses, movable eyes and chenille-stem antennae. Use ribbon or lace for wings.

OCTOPUS PUPPETS Ⓔ

FOR EACH ONE

Thick yarn
Yardstick
4" plastic-foam ball
2 craft eyes, buttons or scraps of felt
Tacky glue (we used Aleene's Original)

CUT 48 strands of yarn, each 36" long.

HOLD yarn strands together evenly. Using a small length of yarn, tie all the strands together at the center.

DRAPE bundle of yarn over foam ball. Separate strands to cover ball completely. Use small length of yarn to tie the strands underneath the ball tightly.

HOLD ball in one hand and gently tug on each strand to smooth them over the ball.

DIVIDE strands into 8 sections (6 strands each).

BRAID sections and tie ends with bits of yarn. Trim excess.

USE glue to attach eyes. Glue a bit of yarn for a mouth.

LET IT SNOW

Watch the snow fall all year with a homemade snow globe.

FOR EACH ONE

Glass jar (from baby food or pickles)
Waterproof glue
Plastic figure
1 teaspoon of white glitter
Tacky glue (we used Aleene's Original)
Fun Foam in assorted colors

WASH and dry glass jars and lids.

USE waterproof glue to secure a plastic figure to inside of lid and let dry at least 24 hours.

FILL jar with water and white glitter.

USE waterproof glue to attach lid to jar to seal.

CUT a strip of foam to fit edge of lid. Trim foam edges as desired. Glue foam around edge of lid.

LEAPIN' LEPRECHAUN

Be Irish for a day.

Sturdy green card stock
Construction paper: black and yellow
Tacky glue (we used Aleene's Original)
½ yard of ½" elastic
Black chenille stem
Small shamrock stickers

CUT hat shape and clover from green card stock.

CUT strip of black paper for the hatband and glue to front of hat.

GLUE yellow square on black strip to make buckle.

GLUE 1 end of elastic to back edge of hat behind band; wrap elastic around child's head to test fit. Cut away excess elastic and glue at the end in place.

WRAP chenille stem around pencil to form spiral. Glue clover to 1 end; glue other end to top of hat.

STICK shamrocks on hat band.

POTLUCK (E)

Welcome spring with some freshly potted plants.

Terra-cotta pot
High-gloss varnish
Paintbrush
Buttons in different sizes
Low-temp glue gun
Fun Foam in assorted colors
Potting soil and plant

PAINT pot with high-gloss varnish.

GLUE several buttons together in a stack to make each eye. Glue eyes to pot.

CUT foam for eyebrows, nose and mouth; glue to pot.

FILL pot with soil and plant.

MY PROJECTS

List all the cool projects you've made that you were particularly happy with; jot down anything you might do to enhance the project if you were to make it again. Include any comments or suggestions to share with friends and family.

List the projects from this book that you've finished. Use the space to add any information you might want to remember about the project or any ideas you have to improve it. Make sure to make note of page numbers for easy reference in case you plan to do it again.

FUTURE PROJECTS

Make a list of projects you'd like to accomplish, or are already planning to do, then make a note of when you'd like to finish them. Use this section for writing any reminders to yourself and to keep track of upcoming holidays, parties or events that call for something special.

HOW TO ENLARGE PATTERNS

On a photocopier, increase successive copies until each grid section is required length. Otherwise, draw grid on pattern by connecting lines shown on edges. On graph or plain paper, make a grid of squares the required size. In each square, copy the corresponding square of the pattern.

WARNING ABOUT DANGEROUS TOOLS

Make sure that all dangerous tools, such as drill and saw, are operated by an adult, or under an adult's supervision.

PHOTO CREDITS

Front cover, clockwise from top left: Paula Hible, David Lewis Taylor, SW Productions/Brand X/Corbis, Tom McWilliam, Paula Hible; back cover, clockwise from top left: Ariel Skelley/Corbis, Paula Hible, Brian Hagiwara, Alan Richardson.

Page 6 (top): Linda Farwell; page 6 (bottom): Joe Polillio; page 7 (top): Tom McWilliam; page 7 (bottom): John Bessler; pages 8 and 9: Tom McWilliam; page 10: Theresa Raffetto; pages 11, 12, 13 and 14 (left): Tom McWilliam; page 14 (right): Stan Wan; pages 15 and 16: Tom McWilliam; page 17 (top): Theresa Raffetto; page 17 (bottom) and 18: Tom McWilliam; page 19 (top): John Bessler; page 19 (bottom), 20–36: Tom McWilliam; page 37 (left): Linda Farwell; page 37 (right): Stan Wan; page 38 (left): Theresa Raffetto; pages 38 (right) and 39: Tom McWilliam; page 40 (top): John Bessler; page 40 (bottom) and 41: Joe Polillio; page 42: Linda Farwell; page 43: Tom McWilliam; pages 44 and 45: Joe Polillio; pages 46 and 47 (left): Tom McWilliam; page 47 (right): John Bessler; page 48: Tom McWilliam; page 49: Theresa Raffetto; pages 50–56: Tom McWilliam; page 57 (left): David Lewis Taylor; page 57 (right): Tom McWilliam; pages 58 and 59 (left): Paula Hible; page 59 (right): Alan Richardson; page 60 (bottom): Paula Hible; pages 60 (top) and 61 (right): Alan Richardson; page 61 (left): Len Lagrua; pages 62–68: Marcus Tullis; page 69: Tom McWilliam; page 72: Anita Calero; pages 73–78: Tom McWilliam; page 79: John Bessler; pages 81–85: Tom McWilliam; page 86: Linda Farwell; page 87 (top): Joe Polillio; page 87 (bottom): Charles Schiller; page 88 (right): Linda Farwell; pages 88 (left) and 89: Tom McWilliam; pages 90–92: Joe Polillio; page 94 (left): Marcus Tullis; pages 94 (right) and 95 (left): Paula Hible; page 95 (right): Theresa Raffetto; page 96 (center and bottom): Marcus Tullis; page 96 (top): Joe Polillio; page 97 (top): Carrie Prophett; pages 97 (bottom) and 98 (right): Joe Polillio; page 98 (left): Paula Hible; page 99 (top): Linda Farwell; page 99 (bottom): Marcus Tullis; page 100 (top): Paula Hible; page 100 (bottom): Joe Polillio; page 101 (top and center): Linda Farwell; page 101 (bottom): Marcus Tullis; page 102 (right): Linda Farwell; page 102 (left): Carrie Prophett; page 103 (left): Marcus Tullis; page 103 (right): Joe Polillio; pages 104–105: Tom McWilliam; page 106: Kit Latham; page 107 (right): Paula Hible; page 107 (left) Linda Farwell; page 108: Joe Polillio; page 109: Paula Hibble; page 110 (top): Marcus Tullis; page 110 (bottom): John Bessler; page 111 (top): Paula Hibble; page 111 (bottom): Len Lagrua; page 112: Kit Latham; page 113 (top): Len Lagrua; page 113 (bottom); Carrie Prophett; page 114: Stephen Randazzo; pages 115, 116 and 117 (top): Tom McWilliam; page 117 (bottom): Linda Farwell; pages 118, 119, 120 and 121 (bottom): Marcus Tullis; pages 121 (top) and 122: Linda Farwell; pages 123: Marcus Tullis; pages 124–125: Linda Farwell; page 126 (right): Jenny Acheson; pages 128 (left) and 129: Theresa Raffetto; page 128 (right): Brian Hagiwara; page 130: Joe Polillio; page 131 (left): John Bessler; page 131 (right): Marcus Tullis; page 132 (top): Tom McWilliam; page 132 (bottom): Joe Polillio; page 133: Len Lagrua; page 134: Paula Hible; page 135 (top): Joe Polillio; page 135 (bottom): Theresa Raffetto; page 136 (top): Carrie Prophett; page 136 (bottom): Joe Polillio; page 137: Marcus Tullis; page 138 (top): Paula Hible; pages 138 (bottom) and 139: Carrie Prophett.